C000319176

Essential
Czech
Republic

by Jos Schneider

Jos Schneider lived and worked as a
journalist in Prague from 1990 to 1998
and was able to explore the country
thoroughly. He is an experienced
writer of travelogues and guides.

AA Publishing

Bohemia was once called the 'conservatoire of Europe' but sometimes even the musicians take a break

Page 1: the Vltava river, for 1200 years the artery of the Czech Republic, runs through the capital, Prague

Written by Jos Schneider
Translation by Mary Boorman

First UK edition 2002

© 2001 Kosmos-Z&K Uitgevers BV, Utrecht
© 2002 Automobile Association Developments Limited
Maps © Automobile Association Developments Limited

English language edition published by AA Publishing, a trading name of Automobile Association Developments Limited, whose registered office is Millstream, Maidenhead Road, Windsor, Berkshire SL4 5GD. Registered number 1878835.

English language edition produced for AA Publishing by g-and-w PUBLISHING, Oxfordshire, UK.

A CIP catalogue record for this book is available from the British Library

ISBN 0 7495 3341 2

Zosmos-Z&K publishers make every effort to ensure that their travel guides are as up to date as possible. Circumstances, however, are very changeable. Opening times and prices change, and roads are built or closed. Therefore Kosmos-Z&K publishers do not accept liability for any incorrect or obsolete information. Assessments of attractions, hotels, restaurants and so forth are based upon the author's own experience and, therefore, descriptions given in this guide necessarily contain an element of subjective opinion which may not reflect the publisher's opinion or a reader's own experience on another occasion.

We have tried to ensure accuracy in this guide, but things do change and we would be grateful if readers would advise us of any inaccuracies they encounter.

Find out more about AA Publishing and the wide range of services the AA provides by visiting our web site at www.theAA.com

Printed and bound in Italy by Printer Trento srl

Contents

About this Book

Essential *Czech Republic* is divided into five sections to cover the most important aspects of your visit to the Czech Republic.

Viewing the Czech Republic pages 5–14
An introduction to the country by the author
The Czech Republic's Features
Essence of the Czech Republic
The Shaping of the Czech Republic
Peace and Quiet
The Czech Republic's Famous

Top Ten pages 15–26
The author's choice of the Top Ten places to see, each with practical information

What to See pages 27–90
The five main areas of the Czech Republic, each with its own brief introduction and a listing of the main attractions
Practical information
Snippets of 'Did You Know…' information
3 suggested walks
2 suggested drives
2 features

Where To... pages 91–116
Detailed listings of the best places to eat, stay, shop, take the children and be entertained.

Practical Matters pages 117–24
A highly visual section containing essential travel information.

Map
All map references are to the map found in the What to See section of this guide (pages 30–31).
For example, Terezín has the reference ⊞ 30B3 – the first two numbers indicating the page on which the map is located, followed by the grid square in which the town is found.

Prices
Where appropriate, an indication of the cost of an establishment is given by £ signs:
£££ denotes higher prices, ££ denotes average prices, while £ denotes lower charges.

Star Ratings
Most of the places described in this book have been given a separate rating:

😊😊😊   Do not miss
😊😊   Highly recommended
😊   Worth seeing

Viewing the Czech Republic

Above: in the shadow of the mining and steel industry in North Moravia lies a rich area of natural beauty near Frýdek Místek

Right: a Czech workman immortalised in a bas-relief

Jos Schneider's Czech Republic

The Statní Divadlo is one of the many concert halls in Prague, where in April the annual international music festival Prazské Jaro (Prague Spring) takes place

Communist rule in eastern and central Europe was on its last legs when I drove to Prague in 1989. When I set foot in Wenceslas Square I realised that this was different from the uniform deprivation of Eastern Bloc capitals such as Moscow, Warsaw or East Berlin. I found the city a tempting gem, a pinnacle of historic splendour. I had already savoured the warm atmosphere of the country on my drive through Czechoslovakia (as it was still called at that time).

There followed eight years in which as a freelance journalist I witnessed the restoration of democracy, but at the same time I enjoyed the evidence of a thousand years of European culture and history. I was also able to recover my energy in the extensive forests and mountain areas. In the small towns and villages, of which the historic cores had by good fortune been preserved – and since the fall of Communism had emerged from their grey facades – the whole of European architecture was there for the taking, from Romanesque to art nouveau.

The title given to Bohemia by an 18th-century English traveller of the 'conservatoire of Europe' seemed to be true; each day medieval church music, operas and symphonic works of such diverse Czech composers as Dvořák, Janáček, Mahler and Martinů were scheduled alongside lively jazz, rock and pop concerts. Apart from famous classical writers such as Hašek, Kafka and Čapek I got to know modern Czech works by authors such as Josef Škvorecký, Ivan Klima and Bohumil Hrabal.

Bohemia and Moravia, as the two halves of the Czech Republic are called, are not only the densely forested geographical centre of Europe, but are also a treasure house of European culture.

A recent example of modern architecture in Prague: the 'Fred and Ginger' building on the Vltava Quay, named after the American dance partners and film duo Fred Astaire and Ginger Rogers

The Czech Republic's Features

Geography

- The Czech Republic covers an area of 78,866 sq km, just over half the area of England.
- The country consists of two regions: Čechy (Bohemia) in the west and Morava (Moravia) in the east.
- It is enclosed between Germany (frontier 810km), Poland (frontier 762km), Slovakia (frontier 265km) and Austria (frontier 466km).
- The geographical centre of Europe is in South Bohemia.
- The highest point is the Sněžka (1602m) in the Krkonoše mountains.
- The country has a continental climate, with warm summers and cold winters.

Prague Castle is the largest castle complex in the world. Dominated by St Vitus Cathedral, it is the crowning point of Prague

Population

- The Czech Republic has a population of over 10 million, with 1.2 million living in the capital, Praha (Prague).
- The population is made up of Czechs (81.2 per cent), Moravians and Silesians (13.7 per cent), Slovaks (3.1 per cent), Poles (0.6 per cent), Germans (0.5 per cent) and Romas (gypsies; 0.3 per cent).
- 39.9 per cent of the population is registered as atheist, 39 per cent as Roman Catholic and 3.7 per cent as Protestant.
- Traditionally Bohemia has been strongly industrial, mainly engineering, glass-making and mining. Moravia is mainly agricultural with arable land and vineyards.

The Czech Republic
The country is officially called the Czech Republic. When the Czechoslovak Federal Republic split in 1993 into the Czech Republic and Slovakia there was no noun derived from the adjective *Česko* (Czech). Hence the slightly cumbersome official title of *Česká Republika*.

Drinking a glass of beer is not a privilege but a right, say the Czechs (▶ 74)

Miscellaneous

- The Czech Republic has for centuries been famous for its health resorts, the best known of which are Mariánské Lázně (Marienbad) and Karlovy Vary (Karlsbad).
- With consumption at 161 litres per person per year, the Czechs are the greatest beer drinkers in the world, with more than 80 breweries to choose from.
- Pražsky hrad (Prague Castle) is the largest castle complex in the world: 570m long and 128m broad.

Essence of the Czech Republic

According to the 19th-century Prussian statesman Bismarck, he who controls Bohemia controls Europe. This article of faith, which has a historical basis, has caused the Czechs a great deal of misery. After Bohemia and Moravia were swallowed up by the Austrian Empire as crown lands in the 16th century, the Czech character (Slav and Protestant) of land and people was bloodily suppressed. Western and Roman Catholic values dominated politics and culture from then on. Only at the beginning of the 19th century did the Czech language and a feeling of unity revive. But the centuries of Austrian domination prevented the Czechs from joining the Pan-Slav movement that was spreading out from Russia. They continued to feel an affinity with western Europe and more than 40 years as part of Communist eastern Europe did not destroy that feeling.

One of the many small rivers in the Šumava, an area of natural beauty in South Bohemia

THE **10** ESSENTIALS

If you only have a short time to visit the Czech Republic, or would like to attempt a really complete picture of the country, here are the essentials:

- **Visit St Nicholas's Church** (➤ 35) in Prague on the left bank of the Malá Strana (Moldova), a high point of Czech baroque architecture.
- **Terezín, a small fortified town** that was used during the Second World War as the transit camp Theresienstadt (➤ 26). The museum gives a gripping impression of life in this former ghetto.
- **The best wine festival** is celebrated in South Moravia (➤ 75), where *burčák* is offered; a wine that has not completely fermented and so – warm and sparkling from the vat – is drunk like lemonade because of its low alcohol content (about 5 per cent). But *pozor!* (be careful!): once in the stomach it matures fast.
- **The spring water** in many health resorts is not to everyone's taste. But in Karlovy Vary (➤ 18) you can also drink *becherovka*, a herb liqueur – prepared from a recipe which is a state secret. As well as an aperitif, the liqueur is taken medicinally (for stomach and intestinal complaints).
- **Wild water canoeing** is an exciting and, for sports-minded holidaymakers, a compelling pastime near Český Krumlov (➤ 16).
- **The charnel house** of All Saints in Kutná Hora (➤ 21, 109) is as macabre as it is interesting: the ossuary is covered with decorations made with the bones and skulls of 40,000 people.
- **Skiing** is very popular and the most beautiful ski area is Harrachov in the Krkonoše (Giant Mountains ➤ 19).
- **The Boubín Forest**, one of the few virgin forests in Europe, is situated in the Šumava, but is not open to the public. In the nearby Šumava National Park (➤ 12, 114, 115) there are the loveliest forests of the Czech Republic, itself the most densely forested country in Europe.
- **Telč** (➤ 24), one of the most beautiful towns in the country, is a UNESCO World Heritage Site.
- **For walkers** the Český ráj (➤ 40, 114) is an ideal area.

The oldest but still the busiest footpath in the Šumava is the Medvědí stezka (Bear trail), 14km through mountain forests and cultivated valleys

The Shaping of the Czech Republic

Around 4th century BC
Celts settle in the region of the present-day Czech Republic. The Romans call the area near the Celtic Boii-stam Boiohaemum or Bohemia.

Late 5th century–early 6th century AD
During the great movement of peoples Slav tribes settle in Bohemia and Moravia.

9th century–1306
The Great Moravian Empire exists in Moravia. The Czech Přemysl princes extend their power over Bohemia and Moravia. In 1212 Bohemia, as part of the Holy Roman Empire, becomes a hereditary kingdom. The Přemysl dynasty dies out in 1306.

1316–78
Emperor Charles IV from the royal House of Luxemburg makes Prague the administrative and cultural centre of the Holy Roman Empire after his coronation in 1355. Germans begin to settle in Bohemia in large numbers.

1378–1471
During the rule of Charles's successor, the ideas of religious reformation of the

Under Charles IV (1316–78) Prague witnesses a Golden Age: it becomes one of the most important cultural and political centres in Europe

Prague preacher, Jan Hus, take root. His followers revolt in 1419 under the leadership of Jan Žižka.

1526–1620
The House of Hapsburg takes Bohemia into the Austrian Empire. Under

Emperor Rudolf II (1576–1611) the Bohemian capital experiences its heyday as a centre of European art and learning. Under his successors there is a collision between the Hussite Bohemian nobility and the feudal emperor. A military defeat of the nobility in 1620 signals the start of the Thirty Years' War in Europe and the end of the Czech nation.

10

1648–1815

When the Counter-Reformation definitely takes hold with the Peace of Munster (1648), two thirds of the population have been killed or driven out since the start of the Thirty Years' War. The Hapsburg Empire is ruled centrally from Vienna, German is the only official language and Roman Catholicism is the state religion. The Bohemian nobility that has been driven out is replaced by nobility from other parts of the Hapsburg Empire. Baroque, the artistic style par excellence of the Counter-Reformation, reigns supreme.

1815–48

The national rebirth begins after the Napoleonic Wars. The Czech language that almost died out is put on record, Czech history is rediscovered. 1848, the year of European revolution, sees the rise of nationalism in Prague.

1848–1918

Czech political parties arise through political liberalisation following the disturbances of 1848. Social divides acquire nationalist overtones: the German-speaking section of the population forms the ruling and moneyed class in Bohemia, which is rapidly becoming industrialised, while the Czechs provide the workforce. In the late 19th century and early 20th century the division becomes so great that the two sections of the population are culturally and socially far apart. In the First Word War most political leaders of the Czech party side against Germany and Austria.

1918–39

Czechoslovakia, which becomes independent in 1918, develops a stable democracy under President Masaryk (1850–1937) and his successor Edvard Beneš. In September 1938 the German border areas have to be handed over to Germany (Treaty of Munich). In March 1939 Bohemia and Moldavia are absorbed into Germany as protectorates. The Slovak part becomes a German vassal state.

1945–89

After the Second World War the German minority is largely driven out of the country. In 1948 the Communists, the largest party in the restored democracy, seize power. In 1968 there is an attempt to restore democracy from within the totalitarian regime during the Prague Spring. The Soviet Union steps in with military support. The Communist order collapses at the end of 1989 in the Velvet Revolution.

1990–2001

The writer Václav Havel becomes president. In 1993 the Czechoslovak Federal Republic divides into the independent states of Slovakia and the Czech Republic.

Tomáš Garrigue Masaryk (1850–1937), by profession sociologist and philosopher, was the first president of Czechoslovakia

Peace and Quiet

Černé Jezero (Black Lake), with an area of 18ha and depth of 32m, is the biggest of the five lakes in Šumava, South Bohemian

The Czech Republic is surrounded by a chain of moderately high mountains. Only in the southeast is it open to the Danube plains. The basin, within which the interior unfolds, consists of a network of softly glowing sandstone hills, with here and there a basalt peak which is often crowned by a castle, sometimes in ruins. The mountains and hills are covered with woodland – in fact the Czech Republic has more forests than any other European country.

Forests

Most forests are in southwestern Šumava. Although the woods in the northern mountains have been affected by pollution from intensive industry and mining, they are otherwise largely undamaged by human activity. Above the tree line there are extensive meadows rich in flowers, while in the valleys there are many streams and small rivers. The Šumava National Park (► 114, 115) and the primeval Boubín Forest are protected areas.

Mountains

In contrast to the neighbouring urban region of Ostrava, which is scarred by mining and industry, the Beskydy region is a paradise of peace and natural beauty. In this northeastern area of hills and mountains groups of ethnic peoples – Poles, Wallachians, eastern European Jews – have settled from ancient times, and many of their traditions have been preserved. These are expressed in costumes, in the timber houses, folk festivals and in the three open-air museums near the small town of Rožnov. The pattern of woods, meadows and fields provides the setting for attractive footpaths. A lookout tower on the highest peak, the 1324m-high Lýsa Hora, offers a wonderful panorama.

State Reserves

Visitors from Prague who long for peace and quiet hurry off to Divoká Šárka on the western edge of the city. 'Wild Šárka' is a largely uncultivated nature reserve with wooded hills, steep rocks and the gurgling water of a mountain stream that winds its way for 7km to the Vltava. Chirping birds drown the noise of the city traffic and the scent of flowers masks the smell of exhaust fumes. In the Chranen gorge, above which are the remains of the ancient Celtic culture, there are species of plants that grow nowhere else in Europe. The reserve is named after the mythical Princess Šárka, who set up a female government in the 10th century in Bohemia and who was commemorated in the third movement of Smetana's symphonic poem *Má Vlast* (My Homeland). Janáček devoted an opera to her.

As well as rocky mountains and dense forests the Šumava also has valleys where small lakes have formed

Health Resorts

The health resorts are places of peaceful relaxation. There are dozens of spas in all corners of the Czech Republic. The hot and/or cold springs, which are beneficial for many physical ailments, are mostly situated within areas of natural beauty. They have been visited for centuries, in the past particularly by the upper classes. You can see this reflected in the architecture and the facilities for recreation: lovely spa hotels, baths, concert halls, terraces, gardens and colonnades. There are now also often golf courses and some cheap accommodation. The most famous health resorts are in North Bohemia: Mariánské Lázně (Marienbad), Karlovy Vary (Karlsbad) and Teplice. In South Moravia Luhačovice is famous.

A winter landscape of Beskydy, North Moravia

13

The Czech Republic's Famous

Jaroslav Hašek

Josef Švejk (left) is often seen as the prototype of the Czech. He is the creation of Jaroslav Hašek (1883–1923), a writer who was notorious for his anarchist views and for his behaviour. His satirical novel *The Good Soldier Schweik* made him world famous. It is the story of a Czech citizen, Josef Švejk, who during his service in World War I in all possible ways short of heroism – but very effectively – manages to thwart his superiors and disorganise the military system. Hašek wrote the novel, which has been compared to *Don Quixote*, after World War I in which he himself – as a soldier serving in the Austrian army – went over to the Free Czech Army that was fighting on the side of the Russians.

Bohumil Hrabal
The 'minor' Czech language has produced a series of notable writers in the past century. The most notable of them is Bohumil Hrabal (1914–97). His work reflects the existence of (in his words) 'the average Czech who lives on the dung heap of history'. Hrabal describes man from the credo: 'Each person is a genius of whom not all skills are made use'. His stories are in the slapstick tradition because they marry tragedy with humour and a modern perception of beauty. In 1964 he was crowned by authors such as Havel, Kundera and Klima as 'king of Czech literature'.

Franz Kafka
Franz Kafka (1883–1924) is Prague's most famous and influential writer (▶ 33). Because German was his mother tongue he is usually classified under German literature, but when Czechoslovakia became independent in 1918 Kafka became a Czech citizen.

Antonín Dvořák

Music plays a large part in the Czech Republic. The English musicologist Burney called Bohemia in the 18th century the 'conservatoire of Europe' and Mozart felt himself more at home artistically in Prague than in Vienna. Antonín Dvořák (1841–1904) is the Czech musician who is the most honoured internationally. The innkeeper's son, who began his musical career in a dance orchestra, was the protégé of Johannes Brahms. He received an honorary doctorate from the University of Cambridge and he spent three years as director of the conservatoire in New York. He composed music shot through with Slavonic motifs. His 9th Symphony (*From the New World*), his cello concerto and his Slavonic Dances are still popular (▶ 47, 59).

Tomáš Masaryk

The President-Liberator – his honorary title – was a learned man. The son of a coachman, Tomáš Masaryk (1850–1937) studied at the universities of Vienna and Leipzig thanks to a scholarship. In 1882 he became Professor of Philosophy in Prague. As a nationalist he was elected to the Austrian Parliament in 1890. When World War I broke out he went into exile and pleaded with the French, American, English and Russian governments for an independent Czechoslovak state. He became the first president and remained so until his death – a statesman with a great deal of moral authority both at home and abroad.

Top Ten

Above: *the Valdštejnská zahrada (Wallenstein Garden) is one of many public palace gardens in the Malá Strana (Lesser Quarter) of Prague*

Right: *entrance to the restored birthplace of the composer Gustav Mahler in Jihlava*

1
Český Krumlov

30B1

náměstí Svornosti 1

Egon Schiele Museum

✉ Široká 70

☎ 711183

🕐 Daily 10–6

🍴 Dlouhá 31 (£)

♿ Good

✋ Few

Castle

✉ Zamek 57

☎ 711406

🕐 Sep–Apr, Tue–Sun 9–12, 1–3; May–Aug, Tue–Sun 9–12, 1–5

♿ Few

✋ Moderate

❓ International Music Festival, end July to early August. Canoe hire, Myší díra

A view of Český Krumlov from the castle of the town – the tourist magnet of the republic

High upon a steep cliff stands the most attractive castle complex in South Bohemia. The splendid medieval town lies at its foot, washed by the Vltava.

After Prague, Český Krumlov is the most visited tourist destination in the Czech Republic (▶ 113, 114). The small town, with its steep winding streets and 300 historic buildings, is a rare collection of medieval architecture. Above it rises the castle. It was first mentioned in the 13th century, at the crossroad of routes from Italy, Bavaria and Bohemia. At the end of the 16th century the Gothic style gave way to the Renaissance. A century later both the town and the castle acquired baroque features. Since then Český Krumlov has been placed on the UNESCO list of World Heritage Sites as a place of ecological and cultural significance.

The 16th-century Town Hall stands at the head of the main square together with a number of town houses with valuable plasterwork and decorative paintings. Near the square, Široká street contains the most important of the many town galleries, the **Egon Schiele Museum**. It contains 50 drawings and paintings by this expressionist painter, dating from the beginning of the 20th century when he worked and lived for a time in the town. On the other side of the main square, up the hill, stands the Regional Museum.

The great attraction is the **castle**, which is reached from the town by the Lazebnický Bridge over the Vltava and the castle steps, from the north via the Budějovická Gate and on the eastern side from the Red Gate. The high points are the richly painted Red Tower, the rococo castle theatre, which is open only during performances, and in particular the Masked Ballroom, dating from 1748 and decorated with murals of life-size, masked figures (▶ 111). Above the former riding school is a wonderful Italian garden.

A music festival is held annually in the castle and theatrical performances are staged there. In the middle of June is the Five-Petalled Rose Festival, when there are historical displays at the castle and in the town. Medieval games are also organised.

2
Jihlava

Gustav Mahler grew up here and used the town for later inspiration. It was once the supplier of silver to European rulers.

🕀 31D2

Mahler Museum

✉ Kosmákova

☎ 28034

🕑 Tue–Sun 9–12, 1–4

🚌 Fritzova

🚊 Sady 9: května

♿ None

✋ Moderate

ℹ Masarykovo náměstí

The plateau on which Jihlava lies is the border area between Bohemia and Moravia. The forested area and friendly villages are ideal country for cycling tours. The town has its former position as a centre of silver mining to thank for its importance. During the Middle Ages it was one of the most important suppliers of silver to the European courts. Its role came to an end with the discovery of the New World with its large silver reserves – the cloth industry then became the most important source of income.

The old mine workings under the town are open to visitors. On the southern edge of the town the medieval fortifications are still standing and the centre has Renaissance buildings and baroque houses, relics of its former wealth. The kostel sv Jakuba (Church of St James) reflects the succession of architectural styles: it is Gothic, has a Renaissance font and a baroque chapel. In the 13th-century kostel Nanebevzetí Panny Marie (Church of the Assumption of the Virgin Mary) there are Gothic frescoes to admire. On the central Masarykovo náměstí is a late Gothic building with a Renaissance gable which houses the Muzeum Vysočiny (Highlands Museum).

Gustav Mahler (1860–1911), the son of a Jewish businessman, was born in the nearby village of Kaliště but spent his youth in Jihlava. In his symbolic works and songs he used many motifs from the folk music of Jihlava and district. 'In the polyphony of my 7th symphony echo the sounds of the forests near Jihlava', wrote the composer. In Znojemská street stands the building in which his father ran a café and round the corner, in Kosmákova street, is the **Mahler Museum**, which contains a wealth of documents on the life of the composer. There is an annual Mahler Festival in Kaliště.

There are no traces of the notorious Arthur Seyss-Inquart (1892–1946) who originated here. Seyss-Inquart later became Hitler's representative in The Netherlands and was involved in the Austrian *Anschluss*.

As well as Gothic frescoes, the Church of the Assumption of the Virgin Mary in Jihlava contains this splendid baroque altarpiece dedicated to the Virgin

3
Karlovy Vary

30A3

Vřídelní Kolonáda
☎ 3224097

Daily

Zámecká retaurace
Karel IV (££)

Varšavská

Náměstí Republiky

None

Diana and Charles IV
lookout towers

Jazz festival, Mar; Film
festival, Jul; Dvořák
festival, Sep.

*View over Karlovy Vary.
On the right, a sculpture of
the stag which Charles IV
was hunting when he discovered the springs*

*Artists and princes were familiar visitors to
this famous spa where they spent their
holidays or sought relief from their ailments.*

Karlovy Vary (Karlsbad) was founded in 1358 by the
Emperor Charles IV after he had stumbled across a hot
spring during a hunting expedition – hence its name. The
12 hot springs (42–72°C) – that have beneficial effects on
the digestion, circulation and rheumatic diseases – are
situated in or near the five colonnades along the Teplá
river, which here flows into the Ohře. The oldest and
hottest spring, where the water rises into the air in a
fountain, is in the Vřídelní kolonáda (Hot Colonnade).

The period of great prosperity began in the 17th century
and achieved its peak two centuries later. Famous guests
included Tsar Peter the Great, Empress Maria Theresa of
Austria and Emperor William I of Germany, Goethe,
Schiller, Bach, Beethoven and Tchaikovsky. The neo-
baroque Grand Hotel Pupp, for which the first stone was
laid 300 years ago, is one of the oldest hotels in the world
and still the fashionable centre. A cable railway runs from
behind this hotel to the 'Diana' lookout tower, which gives
a beautiful view of the surrounding countryside. The
Charles IV lookout tower is within walking distance of the
Hotel Pupp. Sights include the neo-Renaissance Mlýnská

kolonáda (Mill Spring
Colonnade), the Dům
Zawojski art-nouveau
house and the
Zámecká věž (castle
towers), where the
emperor Charles IV
found the first spring.
The Church of St
Mary Magdalene is
a richly decorated
baroque church. A
little way away along,
among a series of spa
hotels, is the small
but beautiful Orthodox
church of SS Peter
and Paul, with five
glittering towers and
art-nouveau painting.
The Městské divadlo (Town Theatre) of 1886 is the centre
of the international film festival each July. The famous
Bohemian Moser glass is made in Karlovy Vary.

4
The Krkonoše

This mountain range forms the border with Poland, with Sněžka (1,602m) the highest peak. One of the most popular recreation areas.

The Krkonoše (Giant Mountains) are popular in both summer and winter

The Krkonoše (Giant Mountains) contain a 363sq km national park, consisting of two mountain ridges with a marshy depression in between. This is the source of one of the biggest rivers in the Czech Republic, the Labe, which flows into the North Sea as the Elbe near Hamburg. The highest mountain in the country, Sněžka (Snow Cap) lies on the border with Poland. The environment has suffered greatly from acid rain resulting from industrial pollution: 25 per cent of the forests are so affected that there is nothing left but bare branches.

The centres of the Krkonoše are Harrachov and Rokytnice in the west, **Špindlerův Mlýn** in the middle and **Pec pod Sněžkou** (Pec under the Snow Cap) in the east. Janské Lázně is a spa with 30 radioactive springs where polio patients have been treated since the 1930s – this was the first place in Europe to do so. It is also a winter-sports centre which, although less spectacular than the Alps, provides all the necessary facilities (► 115).

From Harrachov, in addition to ski routes, many footpaths have been laid out for summer walking. The footpath from Rokytnice to the source of the Labe can be reached from Špindlerův Mlýn, situated at 780m. From Rokytnice, Špindlerův Mlýn and Pec pod Sněžkou you can reach the treeless summit of the Sněžka. You can also take the chairlift at 770m to the top of the mountain. In Paseky near Rokytnice there is an open-air museum and in **Vrchlabí**, the 'Gateway to the Krkonoše', there is an exhibition about the devastated environment of the Giant Mountains.

✚ 31D3

Špindlerův Mlýn

ℹ Špindlerův Mlýn 58
☎ 493234

🚌 Svatý Petr

Pec pod Sněžkou

ℹ Veselý Výlet

❓ Lift to top of Sněžka, Velká Úpa

Vrchlabí

ℹ National park information centre, náměstí Míru
☎ 421474

🚌 Náměstí Mararyka

19

5
Kroměříž

The most attractive garden in Kroměříž is the 17th-century baroque Květná zahrada (Flower Garden)

Haná is the central Moravian region and Kroměříž is called the 'Athens of the Haná'. This beautiful small Moravian town is a UNESCO World Heritage Site.

The town has been twice destroyed and twice restored to its full glory. Since the beginning of the 13th century, Kroměříž has developed from market town to archbishop's summer residence and finally into the special place it is now. On the site of a farm the archbishop of Olomouc built a Gothic castle. After this was destroyed during the Thirty Years' War, Archbishop Charles II of Liechtenstein-Kastlekorn had everything rebuilt in the baroque style of the Counter-Reformation. He made his residence a treasure house of European painting and rare books. These collections survived a fire that destroyed a large part of the castle and the town in 1752. After the rebuilding Kroměříž achieved its prominent position: during the revolutionary disturbances of 1848 the Austrian government fled to the town and the first democratic constitution in central Europe was compiled there.

 31E1

Archbishop's Palace

✉ Sněmovní náměstí

☎ 21219

🕐 May–Sep, Tue–Sun 9–5; Oct–Apr, weekends and holidays

🚉 Nádražní

🚌 Nádražní

♿ Good

💷 Cheap

ℹ Kovárská 3

❓ Summer music festival, Jun–Sep

The castle, its art collection and the associated gardens are the great attractions of Kroměříž. A tour of the **Archbishop's Palace** and the 84m-high baroque tower lasts about two hours. There are beautiful ceiling and wall paintings in the Mansky sál and the Assembly Hall, where scenes were shot for the film *Amadeus*. Regular concerts are held from June to October. The collection of paintings, with works by Cranach, Titian, Van Dyck and Brueghel are among the most splendid in the Czech Republic. Behind the castle lies the Podzámecká zahrada, originally a Renaissance garden that has undergone classical and romantic style changes over the centuries. There is perhaps an even more beautiful garden complex outside the town walls, the baroque Květná zahrada.

The late Gothic Kolegiátní chrám sv Mořice (Collegiate Cathedral of St Maurice, 1260) is one of the oldest original buildings. In the main square are the Renaissance Town Hall and the Kroměříž Museum.

6
Kutná Hora

Kutná Hora was, together with Jihlava (▶ 17), the supplier of silver to Europe, and the king went to live there. It is now a World Heritage Site.

The history of Kutná Hora exemplifies the rise and fall of many towns in Bohemia. When silver was discovered there at the end of the 13th century the town grew from a peasant village to a place of international significance. The king moved from Prague to Kutná Hora, fortified the town with the help of the Italians, set up a mint and had palaces, mansions and churches built. The town provided all the European rulers with the silver they needed to pursue their political, cultural and commercial ambitions. The discovery of the New World with its stocks of silver and the Thirty Years' War ended its heyday. The town slid back into insignificance, a process that was accelerated by a destructive fire in 1770.

The buildings that remain bear witness to the town's former prosperity. Kostel sv Barbora (Cathedral of St Barbara) with its three naves, dedicated to the patron saint of miners, is one of the most beautiful churches in the Czech Republic. At the beginning of the 14th century the Vlašský dvůr (**Italian Court**) stood round the Mint, against which the lovely royal palace-cum-chapel is built. The Hrádek (Little Castle) nowadays houses a **mining museum** from which it is possible to visit the old mine workings.

The suburb of Sedlec contains both the 14th-century church of Panna Maria, and a most remarkable place of interest – the **Sedlec Ossuary**. Since the 12th century, after the abbot of the local monastery had brought a small bag of earth from Jerusalem and scattered it in the monastery churchyard, thousands of people have been buried in the 'holy ground' over the centuries. The bones were stored in the 14th-century chapel of All Saints. In 1870 the Czech woodcarver František Rint was commissioned to use these bones to make a macabre work of art: in the cellar he set up a chapel made entirely of bones. He used the bones from more than 40,000 complete skeletons to make crosses, candelabra, monstrances, an altar and suchlike.

✠ 30C2

Italian Court

✉ Havlíčkovo náměstí

🕐 Daily 9–6

✋ Cheap

Hrádek Mining Museum

✉ Ruthardská

🕐 May–Sep, Tue–Sun 9–6; Oct–Apr, Tue–Sun 9–5

✋ Moderate

Sedlec Ossuary

✉ Zámecká

🕐 Apr–Oct, daily 8–12, 1–6; Nov–Mar, daily 9–12, 1–4

🍴 U hrádku, Barbaroská 12 (£); U Bakaláře, Šultysova (££)

🚌 Lorecká

🚉 Švermova

✋ Moderate

The imposing Cathedral of St Barbara in Kutná Hora with the Jesuit College beside it

7
The Centre of Europe

The Czech Republic is undeniably the centre of Europe. The geographical centre of the continent lies in a forest in South Bohemia.

➕ 30C1 (between Třeboň and České Budějovice

🚌 Lišov stop on Třeboň–České Budějovice bus

♿ None

The landscape near the village of Lišov

In a forest between Třeboň and České Budějovice a small obelisk marks the geographical centre of Europe

Shakespeare may have thought that Bohemia lay on the coast (*A Winter's Tale*, stage direction: 'Bohemia. The sea – coast.') but the fact is that the only areas of water in the Czech Republic are lakes and rivers. The largest lake district is near the small town of Třeboň (➤ 64), where the fish tastes delicious. And when people talk about 'fish' in the Czech Republic they mean carp, the national celebration and Christmas dish that according to Czech cookbooks can be prepared in more than a hundred ways (➤ 74). Almost every village in South Bohemia has its own carp lake, but the most important ones are those of Třeboň.

If you have over-indulged on the carp of Třeboň, you can go on to the nearby České Budějovice (➤ 50) to wash down the meal with the world famous Budvar beer (➤ 75), which is brewed in the town and is not to be confused with – or compared with – the American Budweiser.

A recommended stop halfway on the drive between Třeboň and České Budějovice (just past the village of Lišov) is in the shadow of the 568m-high Větrnik mountain, the Wind Scoop. Walk into the forest on the right-hand side of the road and follow the arrows on the trees. After a short walk you come to a clearing in the trees in which there is a 2m-high stone obelisk, with the inscription 'Locus Perennus, diligentissima cum bella [illegible] quae estum ad Austria et Hungaria confecta, cum mensura [illegible] meridionalium et parellelorum quam Europeam voc centrum. MDCCCLXXXIX' (the eternal place ... the centre of Europe, measured in 1889: 4901' North and 1460' East).

8
Josefov, Prague

Jews had already settled in Prague in the 10th century. They lived in the Josefov quarter, now mainly a tourist attraction full of Jewish heritage sites.

Jews have played an important role in the history of Prague, and Prague in the history of Jewry. Acceptance and persecution followed each other: kings made use of their services and talents but pogroms occurred regularly.

The centuries-old Jewish quarter no longer exists. In the late 19th century the clearing of the ghetto with its narrow streets and alleyways began for health reasons. It became a modern district with an orderly street layout and dignified houses in fashionable early 20th-century styles. Josefov became the official name, after the Austrian emperor Joseph II who contributed greatly to the emancipation of the Jews in the late 18th century. Very few Jews live there now but their sacred places have been preserved.

The oldest Jewish building is the Stará škola (Old Synagogue) in Dušní Street, but according to legend this honour should fall to the Staronová synagóga (**Old-New Synagogue**). Angels are supposed to have flown to Prague with stones from the Temple in Jerusalem in order to preserve them in anticipation of the rebuilding of the sanctuary in Jerusalem. So the synagogue in Prague was called a 'provisional' one. The German-speaking inhabitants of Prague did not know the Hebrew word *altnaj* (provisional) so they gave the place of worship the strange name of *altneu* (German: old/new). Other preserved synagogues are the Pinkasova synagóga (Pinkas Synagogue), where the dead of World War II are commemorated, and the Spanish synagogue that is built in the Moorish style. Opposite the Staronová Synagogue is the late Gothic Jewish Town Hall with its *orloj*: a clock that runs backwards (anti-clockwise).

The most famous monument is the Starý Židovský hřbitov (**Old Jewish Cemetery**). This was in use until 1787 and from 1450 all Prague's notable Jews were buried here, including the learned rabbi and student of mystical teaching, Löw, who created the robot 'Golem'. There are more than 20,000 gravestones standing or fallen. As one writer put it: 'Nowhere are the dead more dead.'

🕂 30C3

Old-New Synagogue

✉ Červená

🕐 Sun–Fri 9–6

✋ Expensive

Old Jewish Cemetery

✉ U starého hřibitová

🕐 Sun–Fri 9–6

✋ Expensive

The Old Jewish Cemetery

Jewish Museum

✉ Maiselova 10

🕐 Sun–Fri 9–6

✋ Expensive

Ⓜ Staroměstská

9
Telč

✚ 30C1

ℹ️ Náměstí Zachariáše z Hradce ☎ 7243145

Castle

✉️ Náměstí Zachariáše z Hradce

☎ 962233

🕐 May–Aug, Tue–Sun 9–12, 1–5; Apr, Sep–Oct, Tue–Sun 9–12, 1–4

🚌 Tyršova

🚉 Staňkova

♿ Few

✋ Cheap

The place looks too good to be true and it is no wonder that film-makers use this UNESCO World Heritage Site as a location.

In the 13th century the lords of Hradec built a fort on the marshy plain, where trade routes crossed, and connected it via a wall to a settlement. This fortification was surrounded by a wide moat – which was not only a defensive feature but also a source of food. Very soon the moat assumed the role of a huge fishpond.

This town plan has remained intact. Only the original Gothic style of architecture has largely disappeared. After a fire in 1530 Zachariáš van Hradec, the then governor of Moravia who had become immensely rich from the silver trade, decided to have the castle and town rebuilt in the Renaissance style by Italian craftsmen on the foundations of the existing medieval buildings.

The beautifully maintained Renaissance buildings with their arcades form the triangular main square. The **castle** stands at the head of this square, where only the baroque Marian or plague pillar – typical of Czech towns of any standing – is somewhat out of character with the design.

The castle consists of two parts: the so-called Water Castle and the castle that was lived in. The local historical

museum is housed in the castle complex. At the entrance from the square is the baroque kostel Jména Ježíšova (Church of the Holy Name of Jesus) that dominates the town together with the Gothic towers of kostel sv Jakuba Staršího (Church of St James the Elder).

Beside the castle is the Malá brána (Small Gate) leading to the English garden on the other side of the duck and fishpond. By the Velká brána (Great Gate), which gives access to the plain near the old fortifications and the new town, stands the impressive Romanesque kostel sv Ducha (Church of the Holy Spirit), the oldest building in the town.

Music plays a large part in present-day Telč. There are music festivals throughout the year such as that organised by the Franco-Czech Academy of Music. An international folk festival is held in the spring.

The main square of Telč is a succession of buildings in the Renaissance style, hence its World Heritage Site status

The main square of Telč, with the baroque Marian pillar on the left

25

10
Terezín

✚ 30B3

Ghetto Museum

✉ Komenského

☎ 92225

🕐 Daily 9–6. Closed
Christmas and New
Year's Day

🚌 Náměstí Česko-
slovenské armády

✋ Moderate

*The garrison town became a byword for
evil after the Nazis converted it into
a transit camp for Jews.*

In 1780 the Austrian emperor Joseph II built the town as a
bastion against German expansion from the north. He
named it Theresienstadt, after his mother the empress
Maria Theresa. Theresienstadt never had to withstand a
German attack. The so-called Lesser Fortress just outside
the town served as an extra-secure prison. The most
famous prisoner there was Gavrilo Princip, who with the
assasination of Archduke Franz Ferdinand started the chain
of events that led to World War I.

Some 160 years after its establishment the Germans
arrived and made Theresienstadt a gateway to their death
factory of Auschwitz-Birkenau. At the end of 1941 they
drove out the inhabitants to make way for Czech Jews who
were assembled here for onward transport. Shortly after
German and Austrian Jews were sent to this transit camp
and later also Jews from other countries, such as Belgium
and the Netherlands. Although trains departed with great
regularity for Auschwitz during this period the population
numbered 60,000–80,000 in a town that had been built for
5,000. More than 35,000 died in the town.

The Germans spread the propaganda that a normal
Jewish settlement had arisen at Theresienstadt. They
permitted a relatively flourishing cultural life to develop
(concerts, cafés, theatrical performances, libraries),
recorded it on film and showed it to the International Red
Cross and in cinemas as evidence of good practice.

Today there is very little to see of architectural
importance in this average small town. The original
population was allowed to return in 1947, but traces of the
destruction of the Jews can still be seen. A historic plan
near the Town Hall shows the route past the buildings and
barracks where the drama
was played out. These are
also marked by plaques. In the
Muzeum Ghetta (**Ghetto
Museum**) documents and
articles from that period have
been assembled, including
drawings by children. The
majority of Bohemian Jews –
77,297 of whose names are
recorded in the Pinkas Synagogue in Prague (► 23) – died
after passing through Terezín.

*A street in Terezín, the
fortified town that became
notorious during World
War II as a transit camp
for Jews*

What To See

Above: the South Moravian castle of Pernštejn has remained the best preserved of all the medieval castles in the Czech Republic

Left: Moravian women in traditional costume

27

Prague

The longest mountain range (Ore Mountains), the highest mountain ridge (the Giant Mountains) and the most rugged hills (Eagle Mountains) close off Bohemia to the north. These mountains slope southwards to a plateau where the most important rivers, the Vltava and the Ohře, just north of Prague, flow into the Labe river, which rises in the Giant Mountains and flows out into the North Sea as the Elbe.

This northwest region has traditionally been the prosperous part of the country. Mining and industry developed here early and it became one of the richest regions of Europe. The cultural treasures in the towns bear witness to this prosperity. In the late 20th century, however, the economy has also given rise to disasters. In the northern mining areas in particular the landscape and the towns have sometimes been dramatically affected.

> *'God was good-natured: in any case frugality is not in his nature; and he smiled: there lay Bohemia, overflowing with charm.'*
>
> RAINER MARIA RILKE
> *Larenopfer* (1896)

———————————●———————————

Left: *view of the Labské piskovce nature reserve, North Bohemia*

PL Poland   A Austria

SK Slovakia   D Germany

Praha (Prague)

More than 90 per cent of holidaymakers in the Czech Republic visit Prague (population 1.2 million). 'Magic' is the adjective applied to the Czech capital – perhaps a slight exaggeration, but there is something enchanting about 'Golden Prague'. Its historical character has been preserved because the city came through World War II relatively unscathed. In the maze of narrow streets and small squares with their abundance of building styles you can imagine you are in a book of antique prints which are now buzzing with modern life.

CZECH REPUBLIC

0   20   40   60   80   100 km

PL

1602m
Sněžka

Krkonoše

Trutnov
Náchod
Nové Město
nad Metují

Hradec
Králové

Pardubice

Chrudim

Litomyšl

Jeseník
Hrubý Jeseník
1491m
Praděd
Velké Losiny

Šumperk

Sternberk

Krnov

Opava

Ostrava

Karviná

Svitavy

Vlčkův

Žďár nad
Sázavou

Morava

Olomouc

Nový Jičín

Havířov

Frýdek-Místek

Hukvaldy

Prostějov

Hranice

Kopřivnice

Valašské
Meziříčí

Přibor

Západné

Pernštejn

Punkevní
jeskyně

Přerov

Rožnov pod
Radhoštěm

Vyškov

Lešná

Vsetín

Třebíč

Brno

Moravský
kras

Kroměříž

Velehrad

Zlín

Uherské
Hradiště

Luhačovice

Žilina

Jaroměřice
nad Rokytnou

Moravský
Krumlov

Slavkov

Morava

Váh

Martin

Znojmo

Mikulov

Hodonín

Strážnice

Bílé

Lednice

Dyje

Břeclav

Trenčín

SK

Bratislava

Piešťany

D   E   F

M o r a v i a

Odra

Nízký Jeseník

Javorníky

Historic Prague's three districts are Staré Město (Old Town), Nové Město (New Town) and Malá Strana (Lesser Quarter), representing respectively the Gothic style under Emperor Charles IV (1346–78), Renaissance under Emperor Rudolf II (1576–1611) and baroque through the Counter-Reformation. The Lesser Quarter, with most of the palaces, is on the left bank of the Vltava at the foot of the majestic Hradčany (Castle). Karlův most (Charles Bridge) connects this district with the Old Town whose former Jewish quarter of Josefov attracts the most visitors (► 23). The New Town, now the commercial centre, with its mansions begins at the impressive Václavské náměstí (Wenceslas Square).

30C3
Staromestske nam 6;
24810411;
www.visitczechia.cz/main-uk.html

31

What to See in Prague

 Mozartova 169
🕐 Daily 9:30–6
🚇 Anděl
🚌 4, 7, 9
♿ Good
💰 Moderate

Above: *the Lesser
Quarter (Malá Strana)
seen from Charles Bridge*

➕ 30C3
✉ Staroměstské
🚌 6, 9, 18, 22

BERTRAMKA (MOZART MUSEUM) ✪✪

In 1787 and 1791 Mozart was a guest in the Bertramka villa
in the Smíchov quarter, which much earlier had been an
important wine-growing area and was known in the 19th
century for its industry. The villa belonged to FX Dušek,
with whose wife, the soprano Josepha, Mozart had
an affair. Here in 1787 the Viennese composer completed
Don Giovanni, the 'opera of operas', and here too, in 1791,
just before his death, he made preparations for his last
opera, *La Clemenza di Tito*. The small Mozart Museum is
located here and concerts are held regularly.

KARLŮV MOST (CHARLES BRIDGE) ✪✪✪

The stone bridge with its 31 groups of statues is one of the
most famous bridges in Europe. It was built about 1350 on
the orders of Emperor Charles IV.

The earliest statues of saints date from the end of the
17th century. Probably the most beautiful group is a *pietà*
of 1859, the third group on the left hand side of the bridge,
coming from the Old Town. The most controversial stands
opposite: a crucifix that the Jewish community in Prague
had to erect as punishment for their opposition to the
Counter-Reformation, including a somewhat anti-Semitic
text written in Hebrew.

The best-known and oldest statue is the eighth on the
right hand side: St John of Nepomuk, who was thrown into
the Vltava after he had refused to betray the sins that the
adulterous queen had confessed to him (*ne-pomuk* in
Czech means 'not a peep'); after his
death five golden stars appeared on
the water (► 77). For centuries the
image of the five golden stars and the
saint have shone on the plinth,
because legend has it that if you stroke
the image your wish will receive the
saint's blessing.

(► 77)

DID YOU KNOW?

Prague owes its name to the word *práh*,
meaning 'threshold'. This is a reference to a
ledge in the Vltava river, opposite the
Vyšehrad, which was used as a ford.

A Walk to Petřín Hill

The walk follows the route of Franz Kafka as described in his novella, *Description of a Struggle* (1904–5).

> *Begin at Kafka's birthplace behind the Town Hall on Old Town Hall Square (▶ 34). Follow the narrow street opposite the Astronomical Clock to Wenceslas Square, then turn right on to Národní Street. Turn right again by the National Theatre and the Slávia café–restaurant. Follow the river to Charles Bridge.*

The National Theatre, opened in 1883, is the symbol of the Czech struggle for independence: the building was paid for by a national collection from the Czech population of Bohemia. Slávia is the most famous coffee house in Prague, a meeting place for artists and students.

> *Cross Charles Bridge to the Lesser Quarter. At the end of Bridge Street turn left and then immediately right and follow Tržiště (Market Street) and Vlašská (Italian Street).*

On Charles Bridge there are 31 groups of statues of saints; the most famous of which is St John of Nepomuk (▶ 32). As an opponent of the reformer Jan Hus he was declared a national martyr after the Counter-Reformation. In Market Street is the Schönborn Palace (now the American Embassy), where Kafka had a flat for a time in 1917.

> *Go past the German Embassy and left via wooden steps to the 318m Petřín hill.*

The hill consists of eight parks. On the peak is the 12th-century kostel sv Vavřince (Church of St Lawrence), the Hunger Wall (14th century), a 60m-high tower mimicking the Eiffel Tower (1891) and the Mirror Maze (1891). On the way up you pass the 12 Stations of the Cross.

> *You can descend to the Vltava on the cable car. Walk south to the Smíchov quarter. You reach the castle via the Strahov Monastery.*

Near the cable-car station (lanová) there is a rose garden and a planetarium. The way down to Smíchov leads past the largest sports stadium in Europe (seating capacity 200,000). The Strahov Monastery houses the National Library. Near the monastery is the stone quarry where Kafka's novel *The Trial* ends with the execution of the main character, Josef K.

Distance
5km

Time
2 hours

Start point
Staroměstské náměstí

End point
Hradčany (Prague Castle)

Petřín offers a beautiful view of the Lesser Quarter at the foot of the hill

Náměstí Republiky
Daily 8AM–midnight
(££)
Republiky
5,9,24,26

OBECNÍ DŮM
(MUNICIPAL HOUSE)

✪✪✪

Between 1906 and 1911 Obecní dům, the loveliest art-nouveau building in Prague, was built on the site of the Bohemian kings' winter palace. This architectural pinnacle of the Czech rebirth houses not only a café-restaurant, but also the only art-nouveau concert hall in Europe. On the first floor there are salons painted by Alfons Mucha (▶ 72). The decoration above the entrance represents the suppression and liberation of the Czech people. It was in this building that Czech independence was proclaimed in 1918 and in 1989 the fall of Communism was confirmed.

Staroměstské náměstí
Tue–Sun 9–6, Mon 11–5
Cheap

RAADHUIS OUDE STAD
(OLD TOWN HALL)

✪✪✪

The Town Hall of the Old Town on Staroměstské náměstí actually consists of a number of medieval buildings that over time have been joined together and enlarged. Only the door, with its lovely carvings, now remains of the original building. The Renaissance window dates from the 16th century. Part of the Town Hall is open to the public: the council chamber and the chapel (both with magnificent painted ceilings) and also the tower.

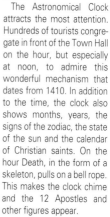

The Astronomical Clock attracts the most attention. Hundreds of tourists congregate in front of the Town Hall on the hour, but especially at noon, to admire this wonderful mechanism that dates from 1410. In addition to the time, the clock also shows months, years, the signs of the zodiac, the state of the sun and the calendar of Christian saints. On the hour Death, in the form of a skeleton, pulls on a bell rope. This makes the clock chime and the 12 Apostles and other figures appear.

The Astronomical Clock on the Old Town Hall is one of the most popular attractions in Prague

The rear of the Town Hall is now a small public park. Until 1945 it was the site of a Gothic chapel and the municipal archives. However, before the German forces left the city they blew up this part of the Town Hall. In the wall there is a stone commemorating the battle of the Dukla Pass in the winter of 1944. The Russians entered Czechoslovakia through this pass. Twenty-seven crosses are set into the pavement in memory of those Czech Protestants who were beheaded here in 1621 by the new Roman Catholic rulers.

The Church of St Nicholas contains many scenes from the Bible and lives of the saints, not only carved and painted but also in the stained-glass windows

CHRÁM SVATÉHO MIKULÁŠE (CHURCH OF ST NICHLAS) ✪✪✪

There are two churches in Prague dedicated to St Nicholas. The one in the Old Town Hall Square makes a sober impression compared with its namesake in the Lesser Quarter, which is one of the most beautiful baroque churches in Europe.

The Dientzenhofers, father and son – the most important baroque architects in Bohemia – built the three-nave church between 1703 and 1756. Seen from the bank of the Vltava river its green dome is impressive, its interior overwhelming. The painted ceiling of the central nave is, at 500sq m, one of the largest frescoes in Europe. There are frightening stone images of saints beside the pillars and the main altar, symbols of Jesuit religious zeal.

The name of Mozart, who according to his own writings 'was happy in Prague', is closely associated with this church: his *Requiem* is performed here every year. This tradition is connected with the requiem mass that was held for him after his death in 1791. According to his first biographer, the Czech Niementschek, more than 3,000 people attended this service, 'from nobles and townsfolk, as many as this great church could hold'.

- ✉ Malostranské náměstí
- 🕐 Daily 9–5
- Ⓜ Malostranská
- 🚊 12, 22
- 🎟 Cheap

ŠTERNBERSKÝ PALÁC (STERNBERG PALACE) ✪✪✪

The extensive Czech national collection of works of art is divided between various museums. This palace contains European old masters from the 14th to the 18th centuries. The most valuable paintings include French works from the 19th and 20th centuries, Italian masters from the 14th, 15th and 16th centuries, German Renaissance works and Flemish and Dutch old masters. The palace, built about 1700, is one of the houses of the nobility round the castle. Castle Square (Hradčanské náměstí), round which it is built, is itself an open-air museum of Renaissance and baroque architecture. There is a lovely view of Prague from the terrace.

- Ⓜ Hradčanská
- ✉ Hradčanské náměstí 15
- ☎ 205146
- 🕐 Tue–Sun 10–6
- 🚊 22
- 🎟 Moderate

Amid the noise of the city, the gardens in the Lesser Quarter, such as the Valštejnská zahrada, are oases of quiet

 Mahlerovy sady
Daily 11AM–10PM
5, 9, 26

TELEVIZNÍ VYSÍLAČ (TELEVISION TOWER)

Prague is celebrated as 'the city of the hundred towers', but the 224m-high television tower in the Žižkov district is hardly a thing of beauty. It is, however, worth visiting this monstrosity, erected in 1985 as a prestige project by the Communist government, because at 65m there is a café-restaurant and from three galleries at about 100m there is a fantastic view over Prague and surroundings. In clear weather it is possible to see almost the whole of Bohemia: to Plzeň (Pilsen) in the west, Děčín in the north, Hradec Králové in the east and Jihlava in the south. The view includes the many towers of Prague itself and the crowds of visitors shuffling like ants along the 'royal route', the route taken by the kings of Bohemia from their urban winter palace in the Old Town to their working apartments in the castle.

Vojanovy sady
 U lužického semináře
8–7 (warm weather) or 8–5 (cold weather)

Valdštejnská zahrada
 Letenská
May–Sep 9–7

GARDENS OF THE MALÁ STRANA

The gardens of the Lesser Quarter, on the left bank of the Vltava, belong to the many palaces that characterise this area. Nowadays they are a refuge for anyone who wants to escape from the throngs of people who stroll along the paths of the aristocratic quarter.

Vojanovy sady is the oldest garden in Prague. It originated about 1250 as a cloister garden, and is now a public park. Above it lies the Chotovy sady, Prague's first public park, laid out in 1833.

In the 1620s the famous general from the Thirty Years' War, Count (later Prince) Albrecht Wallenstein, demolished the district on the left bank of the Vltava to build his palace. The Wallenstein Palace Gardens, **Valdštejnská zahrada**, the best known of the present public gardens, are quite formal. Their paths, sculptures, fountains and flowerbeds are hidden from the outside world behind a stone wall.

In spring, when the fruit trees are in bloom the **Strahovská zahrada** is the prettiest garden in Prague. You can walk along the paths beneath and over the scented blossoms of pear, apple, cherry and almond trees.

Ledeburská zahrada has reopened after extensive restoration. This garden, situated at the foot of Prague Castle, is laid out in terraces. There is an art gallery by the entrance and the exit is through a richly decorated arcade.

VYŠEHRAD ✪✪

Prague Castle, the seat of government, is where history is made, but the Vyšehrad, the hill on the right bank of the Vltava, is where history is kept alive. In the cemetery in the shadow of the twin towers of the Church of SS Peter and Paul, important figures from Czech history since 1860 are buried, including Dvořák, Smetana and the painter Alfons Mucha, who is commemorated in a hall of fame, the Slavin.

Vyšehrad is closely linked with the foundation of Prague. According to tradition it was here in the 9th century that the ancestor of the Czechs, Krok, had a castle built. His legendary daughter Libuše was the first Czech queen and her husband Přemysl gave his name to the first Czech royal dynasty. In the Vyšehradské sady (garden) there are 19th-century statues of Libuše and Přemysl, of the rebellious Šárka and her lover Ctirad.

It is known that in the middle of the 10th century the Přemysl prince Vratislav II decided to build a fortress on this rock. He also had the foundations laid for the striking church of SS Peter and Paul and the St Martin's Rotunda, the oldest Christian building in Bohemia.

For a century the Vyšehrad remained the royal castle. Then the castle on the left bank took over this role. Halfway through the 14th century Emperor Charles IV had the fortifications restored but the Vyšehrad slowly fell into ruin. With the upsurge of Czech nationalism in the 19th century, the old royal hill regained its significance.

Strahovská zahrada
✉ Úvoz
🕐 Daily 9–7

Ledeburská zahrada
✉ Valdštejnská
🕐 Daily 10–6

✉ Vyšehrad
🕐 Cemetery museum, daily 9:30–4:30
🍴 Café (£), restaurant (££)
🚇 Vyšehrad
🎫 Free

Crucifixes are a reminder of the rich Roman Catholic past of the Czech Republic

North and East Bohemia

The mountainous region of the Czech Republic, with its highest peak Sněžka (1,602m), is on the border of North and East Bohemia with Germany and Poland. The Ore Mountains between North Bohemia and Germany have been the economic raft on which Bohemia has floated, historically with their healing springs, and since the 19th century with their supplies of ore and coal. It is now one of the most environmentally polluted regions of Europe. The region of the Iron Mountain, the Giant Mountains and Eagle Mountains that separates East Bohemia from Poland has remained relatively free of industrial devastation. Natural beauty, old town centres and winter sports facilities all attract tourists.

> *'Bohemia has a charming landscape in which the skilful fingers of the Creator have lingered for longer than anywhere else and where every corner betrays His joy over His creation and his benevolent eye. People call this the Bohemian Paradise.'*

EDUARD PETIŠKA
Treasury of Legends of the Bohemian Kingdom
(1993)

———————●———————

Left: *Pravčická Brana in the Labské pískovce nature reserve*

Jičín
Valdštejnovo náměstí
534390
Jungmannova
Tyršova

Turnov
nam. Ceskeho raje 26
366255
Horská
Nádražní

Trosky Castle
May–Sep, Tue–Sun 8–5;
Oct–Apr, Sat–Sun 9–4

ČESKÝ RÁJ
(BOHEMIAN PARADISE)

✪✪✪

Český ráj is an area of natural beauty with fantastic rock formations ('rock villages') and ruined castles in a wooded hilly landscape. It can be reached from **Jičín** and **Turnov**, which are linked to each other by a motorway and a railway line. Footpaths are marked. You will often come across walkers who are looking for the semi-precious stones that are found here.

From Turnov – an uninteresting small town – you first of all see the ruins of the Valdštejn Castle. Further on you come to the rock village of Hrubá skalá, a complex of basalt peaks that stick out above the sandstone layer. The most spectacular feature, visible from a distance, is **Trosky**, the ruins of a castle that was built on top of a double rock formation. The eventful story of this 14th-century fort is told in a museum between the two peaks. If you make a detour from Trosky to Jičín you go through the Prachovské skály nature reserve where the most impressive rock formations are found.

Jičín is a well-preserved small Renaissance town (► 113). It is dominated by the Valdštejn Castle on the main square. One of the biggest battles of the Austro-Prussian War, waged by Chancellor Bismarck to confirm his rule over Bohemia, was fought near the town. It is commemorated by the many monuments that have been set up in the neighbourhood.

A Drive on the Trail of Oskar Schindler

Litomyšl is one of the prettiest small towns of East Bohemia. The brewery in the Renaissance castle was the birthplace of the world-famous composer Bedřich Smetana in 1824. There is a museum dedicated to him.

Drive from Litomyšl along highway 360 to Poličká.

Poličká was a royal town, founded in 1265. One of the most important modern Czech composers, Bohuslav Martinů, was born here in 1890. His parents lived in the tower of St James's Church, where his father was on permanent fire watch. This remarkable home (195 steps) is set out as a museum (▶ 109).

Take highway 34 from Poličká to Svitavy.

Svitavy was the birthplace of Oskar Schindler (1908–74), 'the unforgettable saviour of 1,200 Jews' according to the inscription on the memorial in the town park, made world famous through Steven Spielberg's film *Schlindler's List.*

Drive south from Svitavy along highway 43 to Brněnec.

In Brněnec stands the factory where the 'Nazi-industrialist' Schindler brought Jews to safety from Auschwitz during the final years of World War II (▶ 43).

Via Svitavy and then along highway 35 back to Litomyšl.

DID YOU KNOW?

From time immemorial there have been gypsies (Roma) in the Czech Republic. During World War II 90 per cent of them were murdered by the Nazis. After the war the Communist government brought numbers of Roma, as they are called officially, over the border from Slovakia to the North Bohemia industrial region that had been depopulated by driving out the Sudeten Germans. According to the most recent census 0.3 per cent of the population are recorded as Roma (30,000); but it is accepted that they number at least 200,000.

Distance
90km

Time
4 hours

Start/end point
Litomyšl
🚩 31D2

Lunch
🍴 Schindlerův haj (£)
✉ Pražská 24, Svitavy

Oskar Schindler's factory, where he brought 1,200 Jews out of Poland to safety towards the end of the war, still stands in the village of Brněnec

⊞ 30C4
ⓘ Prokopa Holého 808
☎ 531333
🚇 Podmokelská
🚋 Čs: mládeže

Castle gardens
⊠ Dlouhá jízda
⏰ May–Sep, Tue–Sun 10–5
💷 Cheap

You can take a boat trip on the Labe (Elbe)

DĚČÍN ⚫⚫

From the environmental point of view Děčín is the 'cleanest town' in North Bohemia. This settlement on the border with Germany is divided in two by the Labe river (Elbe). Old Děčín on the right bank has a castle dating from 1305 that 'contains as many rooms as there are days in the year'. There is an old rose garden next to the castle. The Podmokly quarter lies on the left bank. The visitor attraction here is the Shepherds' Wall, 130 stone steps to the top of a rock (also accessible by a lift) from which there is a panorama.

Děčín is particularly attractive as a starting point for a stay in the area of natural beauty in the Labské pískovce, the sandstone rocks of the Elbe that are also known as 'Little Switzerland' (▶ 113). This area is popular with climbers because of its deep gorges and steep rocks, but the glowing hills are also an ideal area for walkers. Pravčiká brána, on the German border, at 30m long and 16m high, is one of the most attractive natural bridges in Europe.

⊞ 31D3
ⓘ Tomkova ul. 177
☎ 5514521
🚇 Puškinova
🚋 Zamenhofova

Church of the Holy Ghost
⊠ Velké náměstí

Gallery of Modern Art
⊠ Velké náměstí 139–140
⏰ Tue–Sun 9–12, 1–6
💷 Cheap

HRADEC KRÁLOVÉ (KÖNIGGRÄTZ) ⚫⚫

One of the oldest towns in Bohemia is situated at the confluence of the rivers Labe and Orlice. Under its German name Königgrätz, the stronghold achieved fame as the site of the battle in 1866 in which the Prussians defeated the Austrians – the beginning of the end of the Hapsburg Empire. A section of the regional museum is devoted to this event. In the 14th century the town was the residence of the widows of the Bohemian kings, hence its name of 'Queens' Castle'. Kostel sv Ducha (**Church of the Holy Ghost**) was founded by them in 1307. It was hit many times as a Hussite stronghold during the Thirty Years' War, which began the serious decline. When the town walls were demolished after the Austro–Prussian War the town expanded (Nové Město). In the Old Town (Staré Město) there is an attractive art-nouveau building in the main square that houses the **Gallery of Modern Art**, which is well worth a visit.

KARLŠTEJN ✪✪✪

Except for Prague Castle this is the most visited **castle** in the Czech Republic. The Gothic castle was built in 1348–57 on a 345m-high limestone outcrop above the village of Karlštejn on the orders of and to the design of Emperor Charles IV to safeguard the crown jewels.

The castle is in three parts: the former palace, the Maria Tower and the Great Tower. The palace contains the living quarters and offices. The Maria Tower was a favourite place of retreat. St Catherine's Chapel was part of the Church of Our Lady; the walls of this chapel are decorated with mosaics of precious and semi-precious stones. Similar mosaics can be seen in the Holy Cross Chapel of the Great Tower, plus five frescoes and 130 Gothic panels depicting saints and prophets. This chapel, with its 6m-thick walls, is not open to the public, since traditionally only the king, the crown prince and the archbishop of Prague were allowed to enter because the crown jewels were kept here. A reconstruction can be seen behind the Church of Our Lady.

Not far from Karlštejn, near Koněprusy is an extensive complex of limestone caves extending to a depth of 600m.

➕ 30B2
🚉 Nádražní
🚏 Nádražní
↔️ Koněprusy caves

Castle
🕐 May–Jun, Sep, Tue–Sun 9–12, 12:30–5; Jul–Aug, Tue–Sun 9–12, 12:30–6; Apr, Oct, Tue–Sun 9–12,12:30–4; Nov–Mar, Tue–Sun 9–12, 1–3
💰 Expensive
♿ Reasonable

DID YOU KNOW?

In spite of official rehabilitation Oskar Schindler, the Sudeten German who was born in Svitavy (➤ 41) and saved 1,200 Jews during World War II, remains a controversial figure. The recent Czech study *Oskar Schindler (1908–74)* tells how from 1935 he worked for the German spy network. In 1938 he was sentenced to death at Olomouc. The Munich Agreement, under which Germany annexed the Czech frontier regions, saved him from the gallows.

Golf is becoming increasingly popular in the Czech Republic

30C2
Masarykovo náměstí
Nádražní Benešov
Nádražní Benešov

Castle
Spartakiádní
Apr–Oct, Tue–Sun 9–12,
1–5
Expensive

Above: *the neo-Gothic
Konopiště Castle, seen
from the sculpture garden*

KONOPIŠTĚ ✪✪✪

This neo-Gothic **castle** near the town of Benešov became well known as the residence of Archduke Franz Ferdinand, tipped to be heir to the Austrian emperor Franz Joseph. But before he could put on the Hapsburg imperial crown he was assassinated in Sarajevo in June 1914, the catalyst for World War I.

Franz Ferdinand, who was more or less banished to Konopiště because of his marriage to a woman regarded as his inferior, had the 13th-century castle restored in the French style and extended to contain one of the best weapon museums in Europe. He collected more than 6,000 weapons from several centuries that are now very rare. A fanatical hunter, he kept his trophies and thousands of stuffed animals are on show. Out of his passion for weapons also sprang his obsession with everything connected with St George: he assembled more than 1,500 works of art and trivia connected with the patron saint of armourers (as well as of England, Aragon and Portugal). The extensive English garden contains many original and copies of statues among the flowerbeds, neatly clipped hedges and ponds.

DID YOU KNOW?

Throwing opponents out of the window seems to be a Czech tradition. The 15-year Hussite War began in 1419 after the Hussites, under the leadership of Jan Žižka (► 50, 65), threw the members of the Prague city council out of a window of the castle. The second defenestration in 1618 signalled the start of the Thirty Years' War: Bohemian nobles threw two governors out of a window of the castle. A third defenestration overtook the foreign minister, Jan Masaryk – son of Tomáš Masaryk (► 14) – who was pushed out of the window of his ministry on the eve of the communist takeover in 1948.

LIBEREC (REICHENBERG) ✪

Under the name Reichenberg, this was the capital of Sudetenland, the Czech region bordering Germany, which had a German population. With its active cooperation under the Munich Agreement in 1938 Hitler was able to annex the region. After World War II most of the Sudeten Germans were expelled from Czechoslovakia as collaborators. Evidence of the wealth of Liberec, provided by a centuries-old textile industry, remains in the town theatre and the Town Hall, which were built as copies of those in Vienna. The museum in the 16th-century chateau at Liberec contains a lovely collection of Bohemian glass, as does the larger **Severočeské Museum**.

Near Liberec is the 13th-century castle of **Frýdlant** (Friedland), which may have been the model for Franz Kafka's novel, *The Castle*.

🚩 30C3

Severočeské Museum
✉ Masarykova 11
🕐 Tue–Sun 9–12, 1–6
🚊 Žitavská
🚋 Žitavská
🏛 Regional museum

Frýdlant Castle
✉ Zámecká
🕐 Tue–Sun 9–12, 1–5
🚊 Čs: armády
🚉 Nádražní
✋ Cheap

Grapes are harvested for the wine produced in the Czech Republic

LITOMĚŘICE ✪✪✪

This town on the Elbe is one of the oldest in Bohemia. Very little remains of the old core, but diagonally opposite the train and bus stations there are remains of the old town wall. On the elevated site where the old Přemsyl fortress stood there is now an empty square with the cathedral. This contains paintings from the school of Cranach the Elder.

Litoměřice emerged from the Thirty Years' War badly scarred. Only the 14th-century castle was spared. The town was rebuilt in the 18th century when it was named as the royal city and seat of the archbishop. Mirové náměstí, the marketplace, is the symbol of this rebirth. The square is dominated by the kostel Všech svatých (Church of All Saints) and the Old Town Hall. A notable building is the Black Eagle, a Renaissance house decorated with sgraffiti. The **North Bohemian Art Museum** houses an altarpiece from the Church of All Saints.

🚩 30B3
ℹ Mírové námřstí 15
☎ 732440
🚉 Pomočné
🚉 Pomočné

North Bohemian Art Museum
✉ Michalská
🕐 Tue–Sun 9–6
✋ Cheap

🕀 30C3
ℹ️ Náměstí Míru 11
☎ 627503
🚌 Bezručova
🚉 Nádražní

Church of SS Peter and Paul
✉️ Česká
🕐 Tue–Sun 9:30–12, 12:30–4
🎫 Cheap

Chateau
✉️ Zámecká
🕐 Daily 10–12, 1–5
🎫 Cheap

MĚLNÍK ✪✪

Mělniti means among other things 'to press'. The grapes that grow on the hill on which Mělník is built are pressed in the town. Emperor Charles IV imported the vine stock from Burgundy in the 14th century, and wine is still made in the region. Mělník rises above the confluence of the Labe and Vltava rivers, a silhouette accentuated by kostel sv Petra a Pavla (**Church of SS Peter and Paul**) and the renaissance **chateau**. The old town contains a square with arcades and lovely Renaissance and baroque gables. You can visit the wine cellars in the castle and take part in wine tasting.

From Mělník you can see the Říp mountain, where according to tradition the brothers Čech and Lech stopped on their journey to the west. Čech remained behind and became the ancestor of the Czechs. Lech travelled further and become the ancestor of the Poles.

The most famous Czech brand of beer that is known in Czech as Plzeňský Prazdroj

DID YOU KNOW?

Plzeňsky Prazdrój, Pilsner Urquell or the world-famous Pils, is a Bavarian not a Czech invention. When the many small breweries in Pilsen were in crisis in 1840 the Bavarian student of brewing Josef Groll came to the town. He used the excellent Bohemian raw materials (barley, hops, water) in different proportions from local brewers and adapted the method of fermentation. The result was a light, clear somewhat bitter beer that in a short time moved from brand name to generic name (► 55).

NELAHOZEVES   ⊕⊕

This small place is known particularly as the birthplace of Antonín Dvořák (1841–1904). His father's former inn now houses the **Dvořák Museum**. An annual music festival is held on September 8, the anniversary of his birth. He is commemorated as a conductor in a larger than life-size statue. In the Renaissance **Veltrusy Chateau** by the village is an impressive collection of paintings by Spanish, Italian and Dutch old masters, which includes a view of London (St Paul's Cathedral) by Canaletto.

On the opposite side of the Vltava there is an 18th-century English garden. In this castle garden there are several ornamental areas such as the Chinese pheasant park and the Egyptian studio.

ŽATEC   ⊕⊕

This is the centre of hop growing. The hops grow in enormous fields, trained up poles, and are harvested by hand in late summer. The hops themselves, scaly unpollinated flowers, are indispensable for flavouring and preserving the most important beverage in the Czech Republic: *pivo* (beer).

For centuries this part of Bohemia has supplied Europe (and later America) with hops. Žatec has this to thank for its prosperity which is reflected in the cultural and historic townscape – now a conservation area. Two 15th-century town gates provide access to the centre with its lovely mansions and arcades. Part of the inevitable castle (13th century) has fittingly been turned into a **brewery**. The hop harvest is celebrated with local festivals.

Situated about 10km from Žatec is the storage reservoir of Nechranice, an area used extensively for water sports.

✚ 30B3

Dvořák Museum
- 🕐 Tue–Sun 9–12, 2–5
- 🚇 Nádražní 🚉 Nádražní
- 💰 Cheap

Veltrusy Chateau
- 🕐 May–Aug, Tue–Sun 8–5; Sep, Tue–Sun 9–5; Oct–Apr, Tue–Sun 9–4
- 💰 Cheap

Above: statue of Antonín Dvořák outside his birthplace, in Nelahozeves

---

✚ 30B3
📍 Pod Střelnicí

Brewery
- ✉ Náměstí J. Žižky
- 💰 Cheap

The Žatec area is the world's largest producer of hops, the flavouring ingredient of beer

West and South Bohemia

West and South Bohemia have both largely been spared the heavy industry that has polluted North and East Bohemia. After World War II these regions were to some extent depopulated by the forced departure of many German-speaking inhabitants (two million people left Bohemia as a whole). And during the Cold War, since they were frontier regions bordering West Germany and Austria, there was little opportunity for development. They have remained rural in character, from Plzeň to České Budějovice, from the foothills of the Ore Mountains via the wooded hills of the Český les and the Šumava to the flood plain of the Vltava.

> *'Before us, in the light of a beautiful autumn day, lay the valley with its villages, churches and castles and, to the right, on the southwestern horizon as far as the Šumava with its darkly wooded hills and towering peaks.'*
>
> JOSEF RANK
> *Recollections of My Life*
> (1816–96)

────────●────────

Left: *potholes carved out by water in the Šumava*

📍 30C1

ℹ️ Náměstí Přemysla
Otakara II ☎ 6352589

🍴 Hroznová hoek 5:května

🚉 Nádražní

🚌 Nádražní

Budvar Brewery

✉️ Pražská

🕐 Mon–Sat 11–4

🍴 Restaurace Budvarka (££)

🍺 Moderate

Black Tower

✉️ U černé věže

🕐 Mar–Jun, daily 10–6;
Jul–Aug, daily 9–7;
Sep–Nov, daily 9–5

🍺 Cheap

**Museum of the Horse-
Drawn Railway**

✉️ Mánesova 10

🕐 May–Sep, Tue–Sun
9:30–12, 12:30–5

🍺 Cheap

Above: *the main square
of České Budějovice
is the largest in the
Czech Republic and is
surrounded by arcades
and baroque buildings*

ČESKÉ BUDĚJOVICE (BUDWEIS) 😊😊

With a population of 97,000 this is the largest town in
South Bohemia. It is famous for its **Budvar Brewery** and
beer (▶ 75). Budvar is the brand of beer most exported
from the Czech Republic, enjoyed locally particularly in the
beer hall of Masné krámy (the meat market) just behind
náměstí Přemysla Otakara II. At 130sq m the town's main
square is the largest in the Czech Republic. (Wenceslas
Square in Prague is actually more of a boulevard.)

The impressive Samson fountain stands in the centre of
the square. The council chamber of the Town Hall contains
a splendid fresco: *The Judgment of Solomon*. The **Black
Tower** rises above the centre which is a conservation
area. Next to it is the katedrála sv Mikuláše (Cathedral of
St Nicholas); the rococo chancel is one of
the best of its kind.

South of the town centre is the
Museum of the Horse-Drawn Railway.
(▶ 108), housed in one of the oldest
railway stations in Europe; the first trains
on the Continent, drawn by horses, ran
between Budějovice and Linz in
Austria in 1832. The museum
contains a collection of models, films
and photographs relating to the
railway.

South of the town is the village of
Trocnov. The Hussite general Jan
Žižka was born here in 1376 (▶ 65).
He led his troops against the
German emperor from victory to
victory until he had lost both eyes.
He was the inventor of the mounted
artillery: canon mounted on wagons,
a weapon that was only copied two
centuries later. He died of a plague
in 1424.

CHEB (EGER) ✪✪

Throughout its history this has been the most German city in Czech territory. In 1167 Frederick Barbarossa built a fortress on the frontier of the Holy Roman Empire. The bastion developed into a walled town known in German as Eger and in 1322 it fell into Bohemian hands.

In the centre of the triangular main square, with its Gothic and Renaissance town houses is Špalíček, a group of 16th-century wooden houses where Jewish merchants plied their trade. The pink Renaissance building **Pachelbel House** contains the Cheb museum with i20th-century paintings. It also houses an exhibition about Count Albrecht von Wallenstein, a general who rose against the emperor during the Thirty Years' War and was murdered in the building – an event that Friedrich Schiller dramatised in a play.

The red sandstone **castle** contains a gem: the Chapel of SS Erhard and Ursula.

🕂 30A3
🛈 Májová 31
🚌 Svobody
🚊 Svobody

Pachelbel House
✉ Náměstí Krále Jiřího z Poděbrad 492
🕐 Tue–Sun 9–5
✋ Cheap

Castle
✉ Dobrovského
🕐 Tue–Sun 9–12, 1–5
✋ Free

DOMAŽLICE ✪✪✪

Centuries ago this was the important town of the Choden, a lawless Czech tribe who during the Middle Ages were rewarded for their loyalty to the king of Bohemia by the grant of the sole right to guard the frontier against Bavaria. When this privilege was removed in the 17th century there was a bloody uprising by the Choden. Their nickname was 'dogs' heads' because they always patrolled with dogs. A dog's head is still the insignia of Czech frontier guards.

Domažlice has a lovely 500m-long main square that gives the impression of an open-air museum with its baroque arcades and stately town houses. It is dominated by the tower of the creamy gold Děkanský kostel (**Deacon's Church**) from which there is a good view over the wooded Šumava (▶ 114).

🕂 30A2
🛈 Náměstí Míru
☎ 725852
🚌 Masarykova
🚊 Masarykova

Deacon's Church
✉ Náměstí Míru
🕐 Apr–Sep, Tue–Sun 9–12, 1–5
✋ Cheap

Above: *náměstí Míru (Peace Plain) in Domažlice*

51

+ 30C1
i Masarykovo 35
☎ 7966164

Castle
◷ May, Sep, Tue–Sun 9–5;
Jun–Aug, Tue–Sun 8–5;
Apr, Oct: Tue–Sun 9–4
✋ Moderate

Aleš Gallery
◷ Tue–Sun 9–11:30, 12–4
(6 in summer)
✋ Cheap

*The striking white
Hluboká Castle dates
from the 13th century,
but was reconstructed in
the late 19th century*

+ 30C1
i Panská 136
☎ 363546
▭ Nádražní
▭ Nádražní

Regional Museum
✉ Komenského
◷ Jul–Aug, Apr–Dec,
Tue–Sun 8:30–12,
12:30–5
✋ Cheap

HLUBOKÁ ✪✪✪

This is a very attractive village but most visitors come here to see one of the most remarkable castles of the Czech Republic: an enormous mock **castle** with 140 rooms in a style that is seen nowhere else in the country. It acquired its neo-Gothic exterior, somewhat reminiscent of Windsor Castle, only at the end of the 19th century when the latest rebuilding of the 13th-century Gothic fortress on the hill above the Vltava took place.

The castle contains a wealth of tapestries, Venetian glass and Delft blue porcelain. The library has 12,000 rare volumes. There are magnificent inlaid ceilings, walls and floors. The former riding school, entered through a winter garden, contains the South Bohemia **Aleš Gallery**. As well as works by the 19th-century Czech painter Mikuláš Aleš it houses 17th-century Dutch old masters and religious art from the 14th and 15th centuries. An interesting aspect is that, since the transformation into a mock castle, the complex has been centrally heated by a wood-burning system.

JINDŘICHŮV HRADEC (NEUHAUS) ✪

This sleepy little town with a core of winding medieval streets offers a sampler of Bohemian architectural styles through the centuries. The large 13th-century castle complex also reflects many architectural periods, its severe exterior contrasting with a varied interior. Several churches in the town contain frescoes, some of them 600 years old.

The **Regional Museum** in the 16th-century Jesuit Seminary in the castle precincts is quite entertaining. Exhibits include *Betlém*, an enormous 18th-century mechanical Nativity scene with moving figures made of wood and plaster in a landscape combining elements of old Palestine with 19th-century Bohemian village scenes.

KLATOVY   ✪✪

Fires have left their mark on this gateway to the Šumava. The 80m-high Černy věž (**Black Tower**) has been burnt out three times since it was built in 1557. It got its name from the blackened walls left by the fire.

The Jesuit church opposite has been burnt down twice since its opening in 1656. The *trompe l'œil* frescoes in the dome are famous but the **catacombs** beneath the church are even more so: they contain a number of well-preserved bodies of notables who died three to four hundred years ago; they were mummified by natural air conditioning. The 17th-century pharmacy U bílého jednorožce (the White Unicorn), which was in use until the mid-1960s, is now a listed building with an **Apothecary Museum** under the protection of UNESCO; the original layout from the 17th and 18th centuries is still intact.

🕂 30B2
🛈 Náměstí Míru 63
  ☎ 313515;
🕐 Daily 9–1, 1:30–6
🚇 Nádražní
🚉 Nádražní

Black Tower
✉ Balbínova
🕐 May–Sep, daily 9–12, 1–5 (Apr and Oct to 4)
🎫 Free

Catacombs
✉ Náměstí Míru
🕐 May, Sep, Tue–Sun 9–12, 1–4; Apr, Oct, Sat–Mon 9–12, 1–5
🎫 Cheap

Apothecary Museum
✉ Náměstí Míru
🕐 May–Oct, Tue–Sun 9–12, 1–5
🎫 Cheap

Above: *the exterior of the 17th-century pharmacy in Klatovy*
Left: *the view from the Black Tower*

30A3

Hlavni 47/Dum Chopin

622474

Hlavní třída

Hlavní třída

New Baths

Reitenbergerova

Daily 7–3

Moderate

Church of St Vladimir

Ruská

May–Oct, daily 8:30–12,
1–4; Nov–Apr,
9:30–11:30, 2–4

Cheap

Chopin Week, mid-Aug;
International music
festival, Jun/Jul

MARIÁNSKÉ LÁZNĚ (MARIENBAD) ✪✪✪

This is one of the more recent health resorts of Bohemia.
It was founded in 1817 and in a short time became one of
the most fashionable watering places. In the 19th century
it was visited frequently by the European elite: the elderly
Goethe wrote the *Marienbad Elegy* here, Wagner
composed *Lohengrin*, and Gogol wrote *Dead Souls*. The
most powerful man in Europe, the Austrian statesman
Metternich, held informal summit conferences here and
King Edward VII and his court were regular summer
visitors from Britain.

The streets are relatively traffic free, the air is fresh, and
Mariánské Lázně is surrounded by forest. The town still
looks distinguished: splendid residences and Empire style
and art-nouveau hotels dominate the spa with its 39
mineral springs. A neo-baroque cast-iron colonnade
opposite the Mírové náměstí (Peace Square) is the centre
of the thermal therapies available. In the Nové lázně (**New
Baths**) at the end of the colonnade, day visitors can have
a single treatment.

*The colonnade is the
heart of Mariánské Lázně,
one of the most famous
spas in Europe*

There is a busy cultural programme in the summer: in
June/July there is an international music festival and
Chopin Week is in August. Twice a day open-air concerts
are given in the colonnade. The Greek Orthodox **Church of
St Vladimir** with its porcelain icon screen and the neo-
Gothic Anglican Chapel is worth a visit.

The Greater Synagogue in Plzň is one of the largest in Europe

PLZEŇ (PILSEN) ✪✪

Pilsen, as the town is known throughout the world, is famous as a centre for beer brewing. But the centre of town is also certainly worth a visit, although it does not seem attractive at first sight because of the heavy industry established by Emil Škoda in the mid-19th century.

Pilsen was founded in 1295 when the king of Bohemia gave the order to build a new town. The town walls round the chequerboard core have since given way to attractive public gardens. Here you find the **West Bohemian Museum** with contemporary art, and the **Greater Synagogue** – one of the largest in Europe (1892). The Gothic kostel sv Bartoleměje (**Church of St Bartholomew**) with its 103m-high tower, the tallest in the Czech Republic, stands on the busy main square. The church contains the famous 14th-century *Pilsen Madonna*.

From the beautifully preserved Renaissance building in the Perlová you can go down to the town's most striking museum: the underground passages that were excavated under Pilsen between the 14th and 19th centuries, with a total length of 11km. They were well-equipped hiding places and storage places for beer; 500m of the tunnels are open to the public. The **Brewery Museum** is at the end of Perlová but the true Pilsner beer can be found in the *prazdroj* (original source) on the opposite side of the river in the Západočeské pivovary (**Pilsner Urquell Brewery**), which was established in 1842 when 26 town brewers began working together. They brought a new kind of beer on to the market, made by the decoction method, strongly flavoured with hops, which in a short time conquered the world (▶ 46, 75).

☩ 30B2
🏠 Náměstí Republiky 41
☎ 7032750
🕐 Apr–Sep: daily 9–5; Oct–Mar: Sun–Fri 10–4:30
🚃 Husova
🚃 Sirkova

West Bohemian Museum
✉ Kopeckého sady
🕐 Tue–Fri 10–6, Sat 10–1, Sun 9–5
💰 Cheap

Greater Synagogue
✉ Sady Pětatřicátníků

Church of St Bartholomew
✉ Náměstí Republiky
🕐 Tue–Sun 10–6
💰 Cheap

Brewery Museum
✉ Veleslavínova
🕐 Daily 10–6
🍴 Pivnice Na Parkánu (£)
💰 Moderate

Pilsner Urquell Brewery
✉ U Prazdroje
🕐 Daily 11AM–10PM
🍴 Restaurace Na Spilce (£)
💰 Moderate
❓ Beerfest, first week in October

30B1

Velké náměstí 1
☎ 312563

Nebahovská

Nádražní

Town Hall

✉ Velké náměstí

❓ Medieval Golden Trail Festival, mid-June (processions, tournaments, fireworks)

Magnificent sgraffito decoration gives the old town's main square its character

PRACHATICE ✪✪✪

As you approach Prachatice and see the shabby apartment blocks you would never imagine that this is one of the best preserved Renaissance towns in Bohemia. The historic town lies hidden behind the old town walls.

The town derived its significance and wealth at the end of the Middle Ages from its position halfway along the Golden Trail: the route over which salt was taken from the Salzkammergut area in Austria to Prague. It lost its royal commercial rights after the Thirty Years' War because as a Hussite stronghold it had lent support to the opponents of the Counter-Reformation. The Renaissance splendour remains and can be admired in the main square which looks like a stage set for an opera. The whole wall of the **Town Hall** is covered with a sgraffito work after examples by the painter Holbein. The wall of the Rumpálův dům opposite is decorated with sgraffito images of battles. The most beautiful painted façade is that of the Prachatice Museum, which occupies the former palace on the main square. There is a fountain in the centre of the square.

The village of Husinec, where the reformer Jan Hus (▶ 63) was born, is a short distance from Prachatice. Hus was burned as a heretic in 1415. His birthplace houses a museum.

A Drive Along the Vltava

From Český Krumlov follow the road south along the Vltava, then from Rožmberk to Vyšší Brod.

Near Rožmberk a castle on a hill is reflected in the waters of the Vltava. Vyšší Brod is known for its fortified 14th-century monastery. In the Vltava here there is an ancient dam, caused by an earthquake, known as Čertova stěna (Devil's Stone), which inspired Smetana to write an opera.

Near Lipno there is the largest reservoir in the Czech Republic.

The 35km-long lake is a popular water-sports area. The most important place is Horní Planá.

From Horní Planá to Chlum.

You leave the tourist area and reach a region where tradition predominates. The Studená Vltava (Cold Vltava) flows into the Teplá Vltava (Warm Vltava). The confluence gives rise to an extensive marshy area, Mrtvý luh (Dead Field), which is a nature reserve.

Via Volary to Lenora.

Near Chlum the road to Volary, for many years an industrial town producing timber products, leaves the river valley. You return to the Vltava near Lenor (glass industry).

Via Strážný to Kvilda.

Teplá Vltava (Warm Vltava) on its way to the confluence with the Studená Vltava (Cold Vltava)

Distance
115km

Time
6 hours

Start point
Český Krumlov
🚩 30B1

End point
Kvilda
🚩 30B1

Lunch
🍴 Restaurace Inka (££)
✉ Horní Planá
🍴 Restaurace Kukačka (£)
✉ Volary

PÍSEK ⚫⚫

This attractive small town was built at a time when gold was still being found in Bohemia. The town takes its name from *písek* (sand) in the Otava river from which the prospectors washed out the gold. The first fixed bridge in central Europe was built here to facilitate the gold trade; still known as Kammeny most (Stone Bridge) it was built about 1250. It served as a model for Charles Bridge in Prague, which was built in 1357 (► 32). In August each year a gold-panning contest is held in the Otava river just outside Písek (► 116).

In Czech cultural history Písek is famous on account of the number of scholars and artists who studied or worked here and also for its printing presses. The **Prácheňské Museum** at Písek has recently been refurbished and is one of the best in the Czech Republic. There is a permanent exhibition of recent Czech history – the German occupation and the Communist period.

PŘÍBRAM ⚫

The name Příbram does not fail to stir many Czechs but the Roman Catholic faithful in particular are thrilled by it because this town is famous as a place of international pilgrimage.

✚ 30B2
ℹ Heydukova 97
☎ 213592
🚇 Nádražní
🚌 Sat Nádražím

Prácheňské Museum
✉ Karlova
🕐 Tue–Sun 10–6
💷 Cheap

✚ 30B2
🚇 Nádražní

Stone steps climb for 400m from the town to the 14th-century Church of the Assumption on the Svatá Hora, the **Holy Mountain**. Antonín Dvořák (▶ 14) was very fond of the organ here, which he often played.

For other Czechs the little town meant hell. The Communist rulers set up a concentration camp for political prisoners who had to work in the now closed uranium mines of Příbram. The town has a long tradition of mining. Silver has been mined since the 15th century. The School of Mines, closed in 1945, was renowned throughout Europe.

Holy Mountain
✉ Svatohorské schody
🕐 Daily 9–6

The baroque church on Svatá Hora (Holy Mountain) just outside Příbram is the goal of the largest annual pilgrimage in the Czech Republic

In the nearby Slivice the last shell to be fired in World War II (a Russian one) is cemented into the wall of the local church.

ROŽMBERK NAD VLTAVOU ○○

This village is worth a visit because of the **castle** complex that stands on a promontory rising out of the Vltava. Originally the fortress headquarters of the Rožmberk family, the Renaissance castle now contains paintings, porcelain, furniture and weapons on exhibition. But most visitors come to the see the Banqueting Hall with its stunning 16th-century Italian frescoes, one of which is even set with jewels.

🚩 30B1
✉ Podzámecká

Castle
🕐 Tue–Sat 9–4:15, Sun 9–3:15
🎫 Cheap

In the Know

If you only have a short time to visit the Czech Republic or would like to get the real flavour of the country, here are some ideas.

Folk festivals are held everywhere in the Czech Republic.

10

Ways To Be a Local

If you greet a Czech with a neutral 'How are you?' (*Jak se máte?*) you might get a full description of their personal circumstances. Better stick to 'good day' (*dobrý den*).

Czech women add *-ová* after the name of their father or husband. Zdeněk Beneš daughter Lenka is called Benešová, but is Mánesová following her marriage to Josef Mánes.

When they go into a house Czechs remove their shoes and put on slippers. There are always slippers for guests by the front door.

In full restaurants it is customary to share a table with other customers.

Do not start a discussion about the Communist past.

Czech players are some of the best in the world as far as ice hockey is concerned and it is a very popular sport. Don't miss an opportunity to see a match.

An empty beer glass will automatically be replaced by the waiter with a full one. If you have had enough, leave a little in the bottom of the glass.

For every drink you have the waiter will put a pencil mark on your beer mat. Pay as you leave.

A feeling for the absurd is something Czechs are born with and it colours their sense of humour.

If you're invited to a Czech home, take some flowers for your hosts.

10

Good Places To Have Lunch

Vikárka (£££) ✉ Prague, Vikářská 39 ☎ 555158. Authentic Czech and international cuisine in the citadel. Book early.

Staroměstská restaurace
(££) ✉ Prague, Staro-městské náměstí 19. Good Czech and international cuisine; 50 per cent surcharge for the terrace.

Adria (£££) ✉ Brno, Masarykova 59. Good pasta restaurant.

Restaurace Na Spilce (£) ✉ Plzeň (near entrance to brewery). Touristy but the best Czech cuisine.

Mikulovská vinárna (£) ✉ Olomouc, 28. října 15. Good meals prepared by the Czech kitchen.

Víno z Panské (£) ✉ České Budějovice, Panská 14. Nourishing chicken dishes and vegetarian meals.

Cikánská jizba (££) ✉ Český Krumlov, Dlouhá 31. Authentic Roma restaurant with fantastic goulash.

Bílý Koníček (££) ✉ Třeboň, Masarykovo náměstí 1. Czech and international cuisine. Fish a speciality.

Koliba Restaurace (£££) ✉ Mariánské Lázně, Dusíkova 592 ☎ 625169. Game and regional specialities. Excellent wine and local mineral water.

Restaurace U Marušky (££) ✉ Telč, Palackého 29. Good Moravian food.

10

Most Popular Activities

Rock-climbing in the Labské pískovce.

Cycling from Telč to Jihlava (35km on surfaced road).
Playing golf in Karlovy Vary.
Caving in the Moravian Karst.
Canoeing on the Vltava near Český Krumlov.
Going to the opera in the Stavovské divadlo (where Mozart's *Don Giovanni* had its premiere in 1787), the Statní divadlo (foreign operas) or the Narodní divadlo (Czech operas) in Prague.
Horse riding in Dvůr Metlice near Rožmberk.
Skiing or cross-country skiing in the Giant Mountains or the Šumava.
Walking in Český ráj.
Windsurfing on Lake Lipno or on Lake Nechranice.

5

Things To Buy

- Beautifully painted eggs, especially at Easter
- Puppets
- Czech garnet (*český granát*), a multicoloured semi-precious stone
- Dolls in national costume from Moravia
- Bohemian glass

5

Most Beautiful Churches

- Church of St Nicholas in the Lesser Quarter in Prague
- Old-New Synagogue, Prague
- Church of St Vladimir, Mariáské Lázně
- Church of St Barbara, Kutná Hora
- Church of St John of Nepomuk in Žďár nad Sázavou

5

Tastiest Drinks and Snacks

- Hot fruit dumplings (*Ovocné knedlíky*)
- *Koláče*: Bohemian pies with soft cheese or plum sauce and poppy seed
- *Chlebíčky*: small slices of baguette filled with cheese, fish or meats, tomatoes and mayonnaise
- Ploughman's: available in beer cellars where you mix the ingredients yourself (cheese, onions, gherkins, paprika, pepper and salt)
- As well as beer and wine, the bitter spirit Stara Myslivecka

10

Best Views

- Sněžka, the highest peak of the Giant Mountains
- The castle hill of Prague, with a view over the whole city
- The Prague television tower from which you can see the whole of Bohemia
- The church tower of Domažlice with a wide view of the Český les
- The Diana lookout tower in Mariáské Lázně with a view over the green countryside
- The lookout tower on the Lysa Hora with a panorama of the Beskydy
- The Černá hora from where you can see the upper reaches of the Vltava
- The castle at Mělnik high above the confluence of the Vltava and Labe rivers
- The castle of Rožmberk with a view over the area of Česky Krumlov
- The church tower of Plzeň from which you can see Prague

Drinking beer is not a privilege but a right in the Czech Republic

30B2

Šumava Museum
⊠ Masarykovo náměstí
🕐 Sun–Fri 9–12, 1–5,
Sat 9–1
💵 Cheap

Below: *the Otava river,
source of inspiration for
the composer Smetana,
flows through Sušice, the
town of matches*

30C2
🛈 Žižkovo náměstí 2
☎ 486230
🍴 Valdenská
🏨 Valdenská

Husitské Museum
⊠ Žižkovo náměstí
🕐 Tue–Sun 8:30–11, 11:30–4
💵 Cheap
❓ Hussite Festival, second
week Sep; Catacombs,
entrance in museum

SUŠICE ✪

In the second half of the 19th century and the beginning of the 20th this town controlled the world market in matches. The fame of the sulphur matches of Schütenhofen (the German name) came to an end when the Swede Ivar Kreuger used the upheaval at the end of World War II to develop a world monopoly of his matches. In the **Šumava Museum** you can learn all there is to know about the 'lucifer'. The museum is on the main square where there are also medieval buildings.

Ten kilometres outside Sušice stands the largest and most beautiful ruined castle in the Czech Republic: the late Gothic tower of Rabí.

TÁBOR ✪✪

This town is inextricably linked to the Hussites. In 1420 it was the bastion of Czech Protestantism. God's Warriors, as the militant followers of the reformer Jan Hus called themselves, made their camp (*tábor*) here and developed the small village into a very attractive town. The narrow winding streets were laid out to confuse any invaders and 14km of underground passages served as shelters and defensive works. The Hussites, who formed a community of equals in which there was no individual property, beat off all attacks by the Roman Catholic opponents of Czech Protestantism, until in 1434 their army was defeated near Lipany. After that the town fell into ruin.

The history of the Hussites in Bohemia and Europe is shown in the **Husitské Muzeum** (Hussite Museum).

Exhibits include the first mobile artillery piece. In the attractive main square in front of the museum is a statue of the legendary Hussite leader Jan Žižka (► 65) and two stone tables that the Hussites used during their religious services. The square also contains the access to the catacombs that are open to the public for a distance of 650m. The Hussite Festival is held in the second week of September with food, drink and costumes from the heyday of the Hussite movement.

Left: fine treats await in store

A quarter of an hour drive from Tábor on the road to České Budějovice lies the village of Soběslav. This former bastion against the Hussites of Tábor has two double-nave Gothic churches of which kostel Panny Marie (Church of St Mary) is famous for its beautiful tower and painted ceiling in the crypt.

Twenty kilometres southwest of Tábor lies Bechyně, a small health resort with an attractive main square and a castle situated on a rock at the confluence of two rivers. The South Bohemia Aleš Gallery has a permanent exhibition about the ceramics tradition of the town, and also holds special exhibitions of ceramics from other countries. The Hačiské muzeum (Fire Brigade Museum) contains old fire engines, and is housed in the former synagogue.

Just east of Tábor, near Chynov, are the caves of Chynovská jeskyně, approached by a walk along a marked footpath from the train station. This stalactite cave is 37m deep and can be reached through a narrow passage. A guided tour, every day except Monday from 9AM to 5PM, lasts half an hour.

About half an hour drive east of Tábor is the 13th-century castle of Kámen. The castle is best known for its motorcycle museum, where models dating from 1899 trace the history of the Czech motorcycle industry.

> ### DID YOU KNOW?
> The church reformer Jan Hus was born about 1372 in the small village of Husinec. He was ordained priest in 1402 while he was a professor at the university of Prague. Humility, simplicity and forgiveness were the fundamentals of his faith, as he preached in his Prague parish church on the Betlémské náměstí. He was condemned to be burned at the stake in 1415 because, among other things, he preached against the sale of indulgences and pleaded for lay participation in services.

🚩 30C1
ℹ️ Masarykovo náměstí 103
☎ 721169
🚌 Svobody
🚆 Nádražní

Chateau
✉️ Masarykovo náměstí
🕐 May–Aug, daily 9–5;
Sep–Apr, Sat–Sun 9–4

TŘEBOŇ ✪✪✪

South Bohemia is the region of fishponds; every self-respecting village has a place where carp can be seen swimming around. In Třeboň and the surrounding area most of these ponds are the size of lakes. Fish – carp, trout, eels and pike – are culinary specialities of this peaceful region.

The historic centre of this spa town is still walled. It has a 14th-century monastery and neat, well-kept buildings from the Renaissance and baroque periods round the main square, which is closed off by the extensive Renaissance **chateau**. Just outside the town walls, on the road to a protected area of lakes, there is the oldest brewery in Bohemia, dating back to 1379.

DID YOU KNOW?
Jan Žižka was born in 1376 in Trocnov in South Bohemia (► 50). He served in the army of King Václav IV. With the Bohemian nobility he sided with the reformation movement led by Jan Hus (► 63). After the death of Hus he became the leader of the fundamentalist wing, the Taborites, and their army. Thanks to his brilliant tactics he won all the battles he fought, but lost both eyes. He died of a plague in 1424.

The Renaissance castle contains a permanent exhibition of furniture, porcelain and weapons from the property of the noble Rožmberk family, which has died out. There is also a display of the history of carp breeding. On the other side of the large fishpond lies the U hrobky Park, a favourite picnic place. There is also a camping area and the Švarcenberská hrobka (Schwarzenberg Mausoleum), burial place of one of the most important, and surviving, noble families of Bohemia.

A number of footpaths are waymarked from Třeboň, the various routes marked in different colours. The green route runs through the nature reserve round the Rožmberk pond – the largest of its kind in the Czech Republic – which dates from 1585. This path becomes the blue route through the Třeboňskó nature reserve that is especially popular with bird-watchers. The red route, about 20km long, goes past ponds, through woods and villages ending up in the small village of Veselí nad Lušnicí.

Opposite: *Třeboň with its many fishponds is the centre of carp breeding* Below: *the Czech Republic is far from the sea, but freshwater fish is very popular*

South Moravia

South Moravia contains the roots of the present-day Czech Republic. In about 830 AD Slav tribes established their first state on the lower reaches of the Morava river, the Great Moravian Kingdom.

Throughout history this southeastern region has looked towards Austria rather than to Bohemia. Nowadays South Moravia, the most agricultural part of the Czech Republic, is known particularly for the beauty of its landscape, its wine and its folklore.

'*The Moravian landscape is gentle and peaceful. From the edges of the towns you look out over the vast fields that show up golden yellow.*'

KAREL TSCHUPPIK
A Son of a Good Family (1937)

———————●———————

Left: this tower is part of the Telč World Heritage Site

A Walk Through Brno

Distance
7km

Time
3 hours

Start/end point
Náměstí Svobod

Lunch
🔲 Hradní (££)
✉ Špilberg Castle

From the central náměstí Svobody (Freedom Square) to the Cathedral of SS Peter and Paul on the Petrov Hill.

On the sloping Freedom Square with its inevitable plague pillar stands the remarkable House of the Four Fools of 1928: four carved figures pulling faces are trying to hold up the building and their trousers at the same time. In Zelný trh (Cabbage Market) stands the elaborate Parnas fountain (1695). There is a very good view of the town from the twin towers of the cathedral.

Via Biskupská Street to Dominikánské náměstí.

In Bishop Street you walk along the terraced Denysovy Park with its groups of sculptures. Kostel sv Michala (Church of St Michael) has a lovely baroque high altar and stands in the small Dominikánskí náměstí (Dominican Square). The new Town Hall on the square has an impressive courtyard and frescoes.

Via the Husova to the Špilberk Castle.

About 100m to the right on Husova Street is the Pražákův palác which houses the 19th- and 20th-century works in the Czech art collection of the Moravian Gallery. The square castle is reached through a broad park. The vaulted rooms under the fortifications are now fitted out as a prison museum.

From the castle to the town.

One of Brno's best known buildings is the House of Four Fools on Freedom Square

Go south past the castle to the old town via Pekařská. On the corner of this street and the Úvoz is an Augustinian monastery containing the Mendel Museum, dedicated to the monk and academic Gregor Johann Mendel (1822–84), 'the father of genetics', who set up his experiments into inherited characteristics here. Towards the north you return to the town via the Úvoz. Past this street, on the corner of Smetana and Kounic streets is a museum devoted to the composer Leoš Janáček (1854–1928).

Detail of a historic building in Brno

Brno (Brünn)

Brno has been the capital of Moravia since 1640. It is the second city of the Czech Republic with a population of 400,000. Apart from its industry and Exhibition Grounds, it is also an academic centre (Masaryk University and Janáček Academy of Music and Drama) and the seat of the High Court. There is an international motor-racing circuit just outside the city.

The historic centre is largely a pedestrian precinct and is surrounded on three sides by parks, the site of the city walls until the 19th century.

Brno was the birthplace of Adolf Loos, founder of the functional style of architecture, and famous for certain modern buildings that were erected between the two world wars. **Vila Tugendhat** by Ludwig Mies van der Rohe – who became world famous as a designer of skyscrapers in the US – is the best-known example. The most famous historic building is **Špilberg Castle**, which has dominated the old town since the 13th century. It was notorious as a prison for national and international political detainees, a function that it acquired at the end of the 19th century and continued until the end of World War II.

Kathedrála sv Petra a Paula (**Cathedral of SS Peter and Paul**, 14th century) stands on the Petrov Hill on the south side of the old town. On Zelný trh (Cabbage Market), at the foot of the twin towers of the cathedral where there is a daily market, stands the magnificent Renaissance Ditrichštejnsky palác which houses the Moravian Museum. The unique **Roma Museum** traces the culture of the gypsies – an ethnic group that suffers some discrimination in the Czech Republic (▶ 41). The city has ten theatres of which the finest are Janáčkovo divadlo and Reduta divadlo. The remarkable Brno Dragon that hangs by the entrance to the Old Town Hall, where the tourist office stands, is in fact a crocodile from the Amazon, presented to the city in 1608. The ghoulish attraction of the **Crypt of Kapucínsky klášter** (Capuchin Monastery) is the display of 150 mummified bodies of monks and members of the nobility in full regalia; they have been preserved here since about 1750.

🏛 31D1
ℹ Radnická 8
☎ 42211090
🚆 Dornych
🚌 Nádražní

Vila Tugendhat
✉ Černopolní 45
🕐 Wed–Sun 10–3

Špilberg Castle
✉ Husova
🕐 Jun–Sep: daily 9–5
💰 Cheap

Cathedral of SS Peter and Paul
✉ Petrská
🕐 Daily 9–6
💰 Free; small charge for tower

Roma Museum
✉ Jugoslávská 17
🕐 Tue–Sun 9–12, 1–5
💰 Cheap

Crypt of Kapucínsky klášter
✉ Kapucínské náměstí
🕐 Tue–Sat 9–12, 2–4:30, Sun 11–11:45, 2–4:30
💰 Cheap

31E1
Valtice, Náměstí Svobody
Valtice, Lednicka

Lichtenstein chateau, Valtice

Náměstí Svobody
May–Aug, Tue–Sun 8–12,
1–5; Apr, Oct, Sat–Sun
9–4
Cheap
Baroque Music Festival,
mid-Aug

Lichtenstein chateau, Lednice

May, Aug, Tue–Sun 9–12,
1–6; Sep, 1–5; Apr, Oct,
Sat–Sun 9–4
Cheap

Above: *the Lichtenstein chateau in Lednice*

31E1
Masarykova
933980
Masarykova
Masarykova

Museum of Folklore

Ottovka
Apr–Oct, Tue, Thu, Sat
9–12, 1–5, Sun 12–5
Cheap

LEDNICE ✪✪✪

The Lednice-Breclav-Valtice-Mikulov quadrilateral is the most important wine-producing area, with regard to quality, in the Czech Republic. Lednice lies at the northwestern tip. In addition, the Valtilednicko – the area between Lednice and Valtice – is regarded by UNESCO as the most architecturally valuable area of the whole country. The noble Lichtenstein family ruled here after the Protestant Hussites had been driven out by the Catholic Hapsburgs. They in turn were driven out after World War II on suspicion of collaboration with the German invaders. But the Lichtensteins made their mark on the region through their buildings.

They have left behind in Lednice one of the most popular and luxuriously furnished chateaux in the Czech Republic. This was their summer palace, built in neo-Gothic style. It has the most beautiful parkland in the country and its winter garden has a collection of exotic plants from all over the world. The striking Turkish minaret of 1802 is worth a visit.

LUHAČOVICE ✪✪

In 1668 a Moravian doctor had already discovered that water from two springs in the forest near the hamlet of Luhačovice was beneficial, but not until 1902 did it become a proper health resort. It is now the largest in Moravia but has retained its rural character. Showpieces and worldly attractions are absent but you can enjoy peace and quiet and fresh air. The Luhačovice **Museum of Folklore** contains regional costumes, embroidery and beautifully painted Easter eggs.

The composer Leoš Janáček (▶ 84), whose bust stands in the park, used to visit Luhačovice each summer in search of inspiration. After a passionate meeting with a woman here he came upon the idea for one of his most remarkable operas, *Osud* (Fate), an opera about an opera that the composer is unable to finish.

MIKULOV ⊙⊙

It is obvious from a distance that Mikulov occupies a strategic position: the castle on the hill stands high above the relatively flat landscape. This small town on the border with Austria was in the dim and distant past one of the first Slav settlements in the region and a bastion of the short-lived Great Moravian Kingdom (830–907). The present town wall dates from the 13th century. The restored houses and churches date from the Renaissance and the baroque. Napoleon was one of the most famous guests who stayed in the castle; after the battle of Austerlitz (1805) he spent a short time there. The castle was blown up by Germans troops at the end of World War II. It was rebuilt in the 1950s and the **Castle Museum** now houses an exhibition of historic and folk artefacts, paintings, and items from viticulture.

🛖 31D1
ℹ️ Náměstí 32
    ☎ 512200
🚌 Náměstí
🚉 Nádražní

Castle Museum
✉️ Zámek
🕐 May–Sep, Tue–Sun 9–4
💰 Cheap

Synagogue
✉️ Husova 13

The 17th-century **synagogue** in Mikulov is famous and has recently been restored. By the Middle Ages Nikolsburg (the former German name for the town) had a large Jewish population led by famous rabbis, including Rabbi Löw, who later became known as the 'wonderworking rabbi'.

Traditional Moravian costume

One of the 'great' Moravian wines, Pálava, is produced at the foot of the hill on which Mikulov stands. This landscape is listed as a UNESCO World Heritage Site, because of the cave in the Turold Mountain, the limestone crags, the rare steppe flora and the ruined castles.

| | 31E1
:-- |
| 🏠 | Seifertova |
| 🚇 | Nádražní |
| 🚌 | Na Brankách |

Caves

✉	Skalní Mlýn
☎	55379
🕐	May–Sep, daily 8:30–3:45; Oct–Apr, daily 8:30–2

| | 31D1
:-- |
| 🚋 | TG Masaryka |
| 🚌 | Durdice |

Mucha Museum

✉	Palčkého 6
🕐	Jul–Aug, Tue–Sun 9–5; Sep–Jun, Tue–Thu 1–4, Fri–Sat 9–12, Sun 1–4
💰	Cheap

Above: *stalactites in the Punkevní cave*

The most famous son of Moravský Krumlov is the art nouveau painter Alf-ons Mucha

MORAVSKÝ KRAS ✪✪

The small town of Tišnov possesses a beautiful Romanesque gateway from the 13th century. It attracts tourists, however, particularly because of its position in the Moravský Kras (Moravian Karst) region. This is a deeply wooded countryside of limestone hills with deep ravines and hundreds of **caves**. The best known are Punkevní and the Kateřinská. You can take a boat trip along an underground river in the Punkevní cave system. The spectacular Macocha ravine, 138m deep, contains many rare plants.

MORAVSKÝ KRUMLOV ✪✪✪

A visit to the beautifully situated Moravský Krumlov is a must for lovers of art nouveau. A surprise awaits in the shape of 20 huge works by **Alfons Mucha** (1860–1939 ► 34), one of the masters of art nouveau, who was born in the neighbouring village of Ivančice in 1860 and died in Prague in 1939. This Mucha collection consists in the main of scenes from Slav and Czech history and differs in style markedly from that of the art-nouveau posters that made Mucha famous throughout the world.

The permanent exhibition is housed in the Moravský Krumlov castle.

SLAVKOV (AUSTERLITZ) ✪✪

This small town is famous under its former German name of Austerlitz. In 1805 it was the site of the so-called Battle of the Three Emperors: the French emperor Napoleon defeated the coalition comprising of the Austrian emperor Franz I and the Russian tsar Alexander I. This Napoleonic success signalled the end of the centuries-old Holy Roman Empire.

After the battle Napoleon visited the 18th-century **castle** of Slavkov to negotiate with his defeated opponents. There is a great deal relating to Napoleon evident in the baroque plasterwork of the salons.

The actual battlefied is 12km east of Slavkov on the **Pracký plateau**. There is an art nouveau memorial, the pyramid Mohyla míru (Peace Monument). There is also a so-called hall of honour containing information about the course of the battle. On the hill of Žuráň near Šlapnice, from where Napoleon directed the battle, there is a stone slab with a map.

🗺 31E1
ℹ Palackého namesti 1
☎ 44220988
🚆 Nádražní
🚌 Nádražní

Castle
🕐 Jun–Aug, Tue–Sun 8–5;
Apr–May, Sep–Oct,
Tue–Sun 9–12, 1–4
💰 Moderate

Pracký plateau
🕐 Tue–Sun 9–6:30
💰 Cheap

Typical wine cellars in the South Moravia wine-producing region of Slovácko

STRÁŽNICE ✪

The southeastern region bordering Slovakia is called Slovácko. The inhabitants are more Burgundian than elsewhere in the Czech Republic and speak a separate dialect. The best-known town in this area is Strážnice. The historic centre is reached through two gateways, the only remaining remnants of the old defensive works. The **castle** contains a **folk museum** with local exhibits. There is an open-air museum opposite with old houses, smithies and wine presses. Strážnice is particularly famous for its annual international folk festival, which takes place throughout the town at the end of June.

Near Strážnice there are many *vinné sklepy, plže* and *vinařské búdy,* separate wine cellars, usually semi-underground, where wine tastings are often held in the summer.

🗺 31E1
ℹ Předměstí
☎ 332184
🚆 Masarykova
🚌 Masarykova

Castle/Folk Museum
✉ Bzenecká
🕐 May–Oct, Tue–Sun 8–5
💰 Cheap
❓ Three-day international folk festival, end of June

73

Food & Drink

Czech cuisine is for hearty eaters who are not frightened of raising their cholesterol level. Meat, preferably pork, dominates hot meals. Fresh vegetables are an exception. Food is accompanied by the local wine or beer.

Beer and Politics

'Drinking a beer with a friend is not a privilege but a right' according to a Czech article of faith, and President Václav Havel, famous beer drinker, believes that beer has a favourable influence. In October 1995 he let it be known: 'I think drinking beer in cafés is good for Czech society because it contains less alcohol than wine, vodka or whisky and with a beer in a café people talk less nonsense about politics.'

Food

The most important meal for Czechs is lunch *(oběd)*. The evening meal *(večeře)* is often a cold meal. Breakfast *(snídaně)* comes into the hearty category. If they do not eat at home, Czechs visit a *restaurace* (restaurant) , a *hospoda* (pub), a *pivnice* (beer cellar), a *bufet* (snackbar) or a *jídelna* (butcher with an eatery attached). Food is not usually served in a *vinárna* (wine bar). *Párek* or *klobása*, hot sausage with mustard or horseradish and a roll, are great favourites and are often sold in the street.

A nourishing Czech dish: half a duck, red cabbage and the indispensable knedlíky

Knedlíky (dumplings) are something special. They are made of flour, and are something like German and Austrian dumplings but lighter. They often replace potatoes *(brambory)* for soaking up the many heavy sauces.

Vepřova s knedlíkem a se zelim (roast pork with dumplings and sauerkraut) is probably the most common dish. A very tasty speciality is *svíčková na smetane* (roast beef with cream sauce and cranberries). Goose *(husa)* is popular in autumn and winter.

Carp *(kapr)* is a national dish. Around Christmas carp are sold live in shops, in markets and on street corners. Stuffed, baked or grilled, they are on every Czech Christmas table.

Vegetarians need to be careful: supposedly 'vegetarian' dishes are often prepared with animal fat.

Food and drink occupy an important place in the social life of the Czechs. Signs point the way to the multitude of places to eat and drink

Drink

In the Czech Republic more beer (*pivo*) is drunk per head of the population than anywhere else in the world: over 155 litres per year. *Pivo* is mainly from one of the more than 80 national breweries, the largest of which is in Prague (Staropramen) and the best known in Plzeň (Prazdroj or Urquell) and České Budějovice (Budvar). The labels on Czech beer bottles indicate 10 or 12 per cent. This has nothing to do with the alcohol content, which is lower in the Czech Republic (generally 2.5–4 per cent) than elsewhere in Europe. It refers to the amount of malt, which determines flavour and shelf life. Roughly speaking the alcoholic content of beer is a quarter of the percentage shown on the label.

Wine is very popular in Moravia. The white wines (including the dry Tramin and the medium-dry Rulandské) are better than the reds (including the somewhat bitter Frankova and Rulandské červené). In addition *burčák* is very popular: this not fully fermented, cloudy wine, has a treacherous effect if drunk too freely. Mělník is the only good-quality Bohemian wine.

Jelínek is the name in Czech of the largest producer of spirits, but the best liqueur is Becherovka from Karlovy Vary and the best brandy Staro Myslivecká from Usti nad Labem.

A country with so many health resorts naturally produces many brands of mineral water (*minerálka*).

31E1

Masarykovo náměstí 35

☎ 556113

Velehradská třída

Nádražní

Staré Město/Great Moravia Monument

✉ Jezuitská

🕐 Apr–Oct, Mon–Fri
8:30–4:30, Sat–Sun
8:30–12, 12–5

💰 Cheap

Slovácké Museum

✉ Smetanovy sady

🕐 Daily 9–12, 12:30–5

💰 Cheap

31E1

Hradištká

Cistercian Monastery

✉ Hradištká

🕐 May–Nov, Tue–Sun
9–12, 1–4

💰 Cheap

Above: *the monastic
church in Velehrad
incorporates remains of a
medieval basilica*

UHERSKÉ HRADIŠTĚ ✪✪

Archeological evidence has shown that in the 9th century this was the most important defensive site of the Great Moravian Empire. About 2km outside the town near **Staré Město** (Old Town) foundations from the 8th century have been excavated, while in the museum known as Památník Velké Maravy (**Great Moravia Monument**) ancient ornaments, weapons, objects made of bone and a canoe are on display. In the town itself the **Slovácké Museum** contains lovely examples of regional folk arts and crafts. The museum stands in the Smetana Park.

Uherské Hradiště is a good starting point for a visit to the white Carpathian Mountains, the forested uplands along the border with Slovakia. In fact the town is in the centre of Moravian Slovakia. There, about 15km from Uherské Hradiště is Uherské Brod where Jan Amos Cornelius, the pioneering pedagogue and theologian, was born in 1592 and died in 1670.

VELEHRAD ✪

This village, a short distance from Uherské Hradiště, was the official capital of the short-lived Great Moravian Empire. Here St Methodius, the Byzantine missionary who in the 9th century preached Christianity in Bohemia and Moravia, spent his last years as bishop. Remains of his basilica can be seen within the present baroque church. The church forms part of the huge klášter Cisterciáků (**Cistercian Monastery**) of 1208, which dominates the whole village. Velehrad has for centuries been a place of pilgrimage. Pope John Paul visited the monastery and church in 1990 during his first official visit to the Czech Republic, attracting some half a million people to the village.

ŽĎÁR NAD SÁZAVOU ⊕⊕

The industrial town of Žďár on the Sázavou river would not be worth a visit were it not for two valuable attractions. One is the Muzeum knihy (Book Museum) in the **Cistercian Monastery** of 1252. The museum has an impressive collection, ranging from medieval incunabula to manuscripts of present-day writers, which provides an overview of the art of writing, calligraphy and printing. The monastery also houses a museum devoted to the architect Giovanni Santini who, with his colleague Kilian Dientzenhofer, gave Czech architecture its baroque character.

The other sight is kostel svatého Jana Nepomuckého (**Church of St John of Nepomuk**). It stands on Zelená hora (Green Hill) above the monastery and is Santini's masterpiece (1722).

31D2
Náměstí Republiky
☎ 28539
Nádražní
Nádražní

Cistercian Monastery
✉ Zámek
🕐 May–Sep, Tue–Sun 9–5; Apr, Oct, Sat–Sun 8–4

Church of St John of Nepomuk
✉ Zelená Hora, Sychrová
🕐 Daily 9–6
🖐 Cheap

The remarkable Church of St John of Nepomuk stands on a hill just outside Žďár nad Sázavou. The architect Giovanni Santini designed the baroque building in the form of a five-pointed star, a shape that is repeated in many of the details (▶ 32)

77

At the beginning of the 20th century Tomás Bat'a made his first shoes on an industrial last. He built up his worldwide Bata shoe empire from this factory

ZLÍN ✪

In 1890 this was still an unremarkable village but one which, thanks to a shoemaker, grew in a very short time to a town with its own special style. Zlín *is* Bata, the world famous brand of shoes. In 1894 Tomás Bat'a began factory production of shoes and during World War I he made a fortune as supplier to the Austrian army. He invested much of the money in the development of the town. Not only did he have proper workers' houses built but also theatres, sports complexes and museums. Obuvnické Muzeum (**Shoe Museum**) is housed in the cellar of the 15-storey Bat'a headquarters. Dům umění (**House of Arts**) exhibits modern Czech art. There are daily performances of plays, concerts and operas in the **town theatre**. It is the home of the famous Bohuslav Martinů Philharmonic Orchestra, and was also the birthplace of the playwright, Tom Stoppard.

Zlín has made a name for itself through the many cartoon films made here. The Velké kino (Grand Cinema), which seats over 2000, is a reflection of this industry. The local castle in Sad Svobody (Freedom Park) houses the Regional Museum where traditional musical instruments and tools from Moravia are on exhibition. There is also a permanent exhibition of contemporary Czech painting and sculpture.

✚ 31E1
ℹ Náměstí Míru
☎ 7214138
🚍 Gahurova
🚍 Gahurova

Shoe Museum
✉ Třída Tomáše Bati
🕐 Thu–Sun 10–12, 1–5
💰 Cheap

House of Arts
✉ TG Masaryka
🕐 Tue–Sun 9–5
💰 Cheap

Town theatre
✉ Divadelní

ZNOJMO (ZNAIM) ✪✪

This is one of the ancient villages along the border with Austria. Fortifications were built in the 7th century and remains of the old stronghold can still be found. Other archeological finds are displayed in the Jihomoravské muzeum (**South Moravian Museum**).

Znojmo had its heyday after the Thirty Years' War. Under the Treaty of Znaim (the German name) concluded in 1628 the Austrian Hapsburgs acquired the hereditary monarchy of Bohemia and Moravia, which was to last until 1918. The town was famous for its wine, the vineyards being adjacent to the Austrian wine regions. Many religious buildings were erected, the most impressive of which is the **Premonstratensian Monastery** just outside the town. The tower of kostel sv Michala (Church of St Michael) is the highest point of the old town, while the best frescoes are in kostel sv Jana Křtitele (Church of St John the Baptist). The baroque salon of the castle of Znojmo has medieval frescoes. Rotunda sv Kateřiny (**Rotunda of St Catherine**), one of the oldest Romanesque buildings in the Czech Republic, forms part of the castle complex. The entrance to the catacombs is in Slepiči trh (Chicken Market). They consist of 27km of underground passages that were

🔲 31D1
ℹ️ Obrokova ul. 10
    ☎ 222552
🚆 Tovární
🚌 17: listopadu

South Moravian Museum
✉️ Náměstí TG Masaryka
🕐 Daily 9–12, 12:30–5
✋ Cheap

Premonstratensian Monastery
✉️ Louká
🕐 Tue–Sun 9–12, 1–5
✋ Cheap

Rotunda of St Catherine
✉️ Přemyslovců
🕐 Tue–Sun 9–4
✋ Cheap

excavated in the 14th century to connect the many storage cellars but were also used for defence. Only parts are open to the public.

Znojmo is famous for its gherkins which are grown here in huge quantities and can be bought as pickles.

The area around Znojmo is famous for its gherkins

North Moravia

The notoriety of the largest town in this region frightens off many people. Except for the Black Triangle of North Bohemia, Ostrava and its surroundings is the part of the Czech Republic most heavily polluted by mining and heavy industry. But North Moravia is more than the extensive conglomeration of Ostrava. There is the gentle area of the Beskydy hills; there is the wildest mountain of the Czech Republic, Hruby Jesenik; and there are the fertile river valleys of the Morava and Bečva. It is also a region where non Czech-speaking peoples settled: Poles, Ukrainians and Jews fleeing from the pogroms in tsarist Russia. The most notable of these ethnic groups are the Valašsky (Wallachians) who preserve their own culture in open-air museums and folk festivals.

> *'The inhabitants approach strangers with an unbelievable humanity, which is something I was able to experience when I was among them.'*
>
> SAMUEL LEWKENOR
> (1600)

———————— • ————————

Left: *the Town Hall in Olomouc, which has an astronomical clock*

🗺 31F2
📍 nam. Svobody 6
☎ 646888
🚉 Nádražní

Beskydy Museum
✉ Zámecka náměstí
🕐 Tue–Sun 9–12, 1–5
💵 Cheap

Church of SS John and Paul
✉ Janáčková
🕐 Daily 9–6
💵 Cheap

The burial ground of Frýdek-Místek, close to one of the town's reservoirs

FRÝDEK-MÍSTEK ✪

Traditionally this twin town, formed by the merging of Frýdek and Místek in 1943, was an industrial centre and intersection of routes. The route from Austria to Poland runs through it and meets the road from the North Moravia industrial region to Slovakia. The textile industry, which still exists, was for centuries the most important source of income, while in recent history metal industries and coal mining have developed. In Staříč just outside the town you can go down a coal mine.

Frýdek-Místek region is popular as a holiday centre because of its proximity to the Beskydy (► 12) and three reservoirs that have developed into centres for water sports (► 115). The town itself has several interesting historic buildings: the 14th-century castle in the centre of the town that contains the **Beskydy Museum**, wooden houses, and the Gothic church of St John the Baptist. One of the most attractive churches is the rococo jewel, the **Church of SS John and Paul**.

Bedřich-Smetana Park contains a number of sculptures. These include a remarkable monument made of slabs of rock that was inspired by the cycle of poems *Silesian Songs* by one of the most important modern poets in Czech literature, Petr Bežruč. He was born locally, and his laments for the sad lot of the Silesian textile workers in the 19th century have also been set to music many times by composers. Bežruč is among those commemorated in the local museum.

In July each year there is a festival of esoteric and meditative music in the Frýdek-Místek museum. In the small town of Brušperk 10km west of the town a festival of children's choirs is held each April.

HRANICE   ○○

The name means 'frontier' because in the past this was the frontier town between Moravia and Silesia. It lay on the ancient central European route, the so called amber trail of southern Europe to the Baltic Sea, which here ran through the Moravian Gate, the lowest pass of the northern mountain ridge of Moravia.

The Gothic fortress that stood here was developed in the 17th century into an elegant castle with valuable plaster-work. At the same time the Town Hall was erected on the foundations of the town walls and the baroque Church of St John the Baptist was built.

⊞ 31E2
🛈 Pernstejnske náměstí 1
  ☎ 272276
🚌 Potoční
🚊 Juriková

Hranice came to fame in the 19th century as the training centre for the Austrian cavalry. Famous members of the Military Riding School at Hranice, then known as Märisch Weißkirchen, include the poet Rainer Maria Rilke, the writer Robert Musil and the film director Josef von Sternberg. The best-known novel by Joseph Roth, *Radetsky March*, is largely set in Hranice. The barracks that have been described many times lie just outside the town and are still in use.

HUKVALDY ✪✪✪

This beautiful village, surrounded by hills and woods, attracts visitors not simply because of its setting. Here in 1854 the composer Leoš Janáček was born, son of the village schoolmaster. By the time he died here in 1928 he had become famous all over the world. His birthplace stands at the foot of the woodland path leading to the ruins of a 13th-century castle. In the lower part of the village Janáček's last home is furnished as it was in his time. The **Janáček Museum** greets visitors with music by the composer, which make clear, through the melodic themes and tone colours, why he is regarded as the outstanding Moravian composer. An annual music festival in Janáček's honour is held in the village, in the open-air theatre situated in a wildlife park round the ruined castle.

31F2

Janáček Museum
✉ Podoboří 79
🕐 Jun–Aug, Tue–Sun 10–12, 2–4; Apr–May, Sep–Oct, Sat–Sun only
❓ Janáček Summer Festival, June

A ruined castle rises above the wooded surroundings of Hukvaldy

31F2
ℹ Obrancu miru 368
☎ 821600
🚉 Nádražní
🚉 Nádražní

Tatra Museum
✉ Zahumenní
🕐 Tue–Sun 9–12, 1–5
💰 Cheap

KOPŘIVNICE ✪

This is a magnet for lovers of old vehicles. It is the home of the Tatra factory, which was particularly known for the manufacture of heavy goods vehicles and buses. During the Communist era Tatra cars were exclusively for the use of high-ranking police, party bosses and diplomats. The **Tatra Museum** contains examples of all the models produced since 1897.

Emil Zátopek, the remarkable long-distance runner who won several gold medals in the 1948 and 1952 Olympics and was nicknamed the 'locomotive', was born here. A long-overdue Zátopek museum is expected soon.

Left: *The Chapel of St Jan Sarkander* (► 88)
Below: *one of the baroque fountains of Olomouc*

OLOMOUC ✪✪✪

As far as the historic centre is concerned, this is the most beautiful town in North Moravia. Olomouc was for many years the capital of Moravia until Swedish troops set fire to it during the Thirty Years' War. Since then Brno (► 69) has been the administrative centre. Olomouc has remained the seat of the archbishop of Moravia, a role that it took over from Velehrad (► 76), which fell into ruin after the fall of the Great Moravian Empire.

According to legend, the town was founded by Julius Caesar, hence the fountain with the Roman general on horseback in Horní náměstí (Upper Square). This is one of the six baroque fountains of Olomouc, a unique group with which the leaders of the Counter-Reformation – the Jesuits – put their mark on a town that they regarded as their Bohemian bulwark. Also in Upper Square is the beautiful 14th-century **Town Hall** with the adjacent astronomical clock (► 80, 88).

It has been shown that in the 11th century a fortress was built on the upper part of the Morava river; as well as the Moravian vassal of the Bohemian king, the bishop of Moravia also took up residence there. In the small Václavské náměstí – former castle square – stand the loveliest historic buildings: dóm sv Václava (Cathedral of St Wenceslas), Přemyslovský palác (**Palace of the Přemyslids**) and kaple sv Anny (Chapel of St Anne). The former Benedictine monastery of 1078 is at the foot of the castle hill on the River Morava. The complex, known as the Moravian Escorial, is now used a military hospital.

Whereas the Archbishop's Palace is impressive because of its sheer size, kostel sv Michala (**Church of St Michael**) is notable for its green dome and its baroque interior.

Parks have been laid out on the east and west sides of the town on the site of the old town walls. Near the southwestern Smetana Park are a number of art-nouveau houses (circa 1900).

About 15km north of Olomouc is the town of Šternberk. Apart from its medieval castle and clock museum it is also known for the annual European championship for vintage cars.

🕂 31E2
🛈 Horní náměstí
☎ 5513385
🕐 Daily 9–7
🚍 Jeremenkova
🚉 Jeremenkova

Town Hall
✉ Horní náměstí
🕐 Mar–Oct: daily 11–11:30, 3–5
↔ Astronomical clock (► 80, 88)

Palace of the Přemyslids
✉ Václavské náměstí
🕐 Tue–Sun 9–12, 1–5
✋ Cheap

Church of St Michael
✉ Panská
🕐 Daily 9–6
✋ Cheap

31E2

Horní náměstí 67

☎ 621140

Janška

Janška/Husova

Silesian Museum

✉ Tyršova 1

🕐 Tue–Sun 9–12, 1:30–5

💰 Cheap

Above: the beautiful building of the Silesian Museum in Opava

31F2

Nádražní 7

☎ 6123913

28: Řijna

28: Řijna

Old Town Hall

✉ Masarykovo náměstí

🕐 Mon–Fri 9–5, Sat–Sun 9–1

💰 Cheap

Church of St Catherine

✉ Hrabůvka

🕐 Sun–Fri 9–12, 1–5, Sat 9–12

OPAVA (TROPPAU) ✪

The 800-year-old town was for centuries the capital of Austrian Silesia and the Czech region of Slezko that became part of Moravia in 1928. There is, however, very little to see of this administrative and cultural past. At the end of the World War II Opava, which had traditionally been populated by Sudeten Germans, suffered heavy bombardment.

The well laid-out **Silesian Museum** gives great insight into the history of the town and its hinterland. The Knights of the German Order – members of the North German nobility who since the crusades had defended Christianity with fire and sword but who also founded hospitals and cared for the poor – played a large part.

On nám 1máje (1st May Square) a Gothic tower that was once a warehouse is now part of the Town Hall.

Opava is a very good starting point for excursions to the Jeseníky Mountains.

OSTRAVA ✪

The authorities are doing their best, but they are never going to turn this sprawling industrial town into the attractive small provincial town it once was. Towns and villages have been absorbed into a conurbation with a population of 328,500 – the third city in the Czech Republic. For the Communist rulers it was a model for their workers' paradise. Smoking factory chimneys, steaming blast furnaces and the rusting winding gear of mine shafts still dominate the cityscape. The ugly face of Moravia, but with a good heart; the small historic centre with its Renaissance architecture gives a touch of distinction. Kostel sv Václava (Church of St Wenceslas), the **Old Town Hall**, chrám Božského Spasitele (Church of the Divine Saviour) and the art-nouveau theatre are worth visiting, as is the wooden kostel sv Kateřiny (**Church of St Catherine**) in the Hrabová district. However, after a day the nearby Beskydy hills (➤ 12) beckon.

PŘÍBOR ✪

A number of historic buildings stand in the centre of this small town, which until the World War II was of regional significance because of the Renaissance college, a training centre for teachers. There is a square with 16th-century houses and arcades, a Gothic church from the 14th century, an 18th-century baroque church and the remains of the town's fortifications.

The most important building is, however, a small house just outside the centre. In this building, with the inscription *A. Žávic*, Sigmund Freud was born in 1856 to Jewish parents, who had exchanged the turbulent Ukraine for the peace of North Moravia's countryside. His birthplace now houses a **Freud Museum**, where the emphasis is on the early years of the founder of psychoanalysis.

🚹 31F2
🏛 Náměstí Svobody

Freud Museum
✉ Hlavní

ROŽNOV POD RADHOŠTĚM ✪✪

The area in which Rožnov is situated is also known as Valašsko, because in the 15th century a tribe of shepherds settled there and it has never been clear where they came from. They are known as Valach (*valaška* means shepherd's crook) or Wallachians. There are still signs of their culture: in Rožnov they have been assembled in the **Wallachian Open-air Museum**, where the traditional life and work of this mysterious people can be seen in three sections: the Wooden Hamlet, the Wallachian Shepherds' Village, and the Mill Valley. The buildings and tools are authentic, collected from all corners of Valašsko. During holiday periods Rožnov hosts a rolling programme of folk festivals, especially at weekends.

Rožnov lies at the foot of the 1,129m-high Radhošt. From the open-air museum an 8km trail is marked out to the summit from which you have a wonderful view of the area.

🚹 31F2
ℹ Palackeho 484
☎ 655196
🚃 Nádražní
🚌 Nádražní

Wallachian Open-air Museum
✉ Palackého
🕐 May–Oct, daily 9–5
Moderate
❓ Folk Festivals, Jun, Jul, Aug

Musicians play folk music in the Wallachian Open-air Museum at Rožnov

A Walk Through Olomouc

Distance
3km

Time
2 hours

Start/End point
Horní náměstí

Lunch
Karvárna Terasa (£)
Křížovského 5

From Horní náměstí to Dolní náměstí.

The beautiful Town Hall, 1378, stands in Upper Square. On the north side there is an astronomical clock, which was the Communist answer to the astronomical clock on the Town Hall in Prague; in Olomouc, instead of saints, a procession of wooden proletarians appear every hour. Apart from two fountains the square has the largest baroque plague pillar in the Czech Republic, the Trinity Column.

Lower Square, Dolní náměstí, also has two fountains and a plague pillar. The plain kostel Zvěstování Panny Marie (Church of the Annunciation) stands out with its sobriety and simple interior.

Via Panská to Václavské náměstí.

Through narrow streets you arrive at St Michael's Church (► 85). On the corner of Na hradě (to the castle) is the chapel of St Jan Sarkander one of the most controversial saints in the Czech Republic, because he was a notorious persecutor of the Hussites. Past the Jesuit Church of Panny Marie Sněžné (St Mary of the Snows), richly decorated with frescoes, you reach Palacký University, once a Jesuit college. From there you reach the Archbishop's Palace via Václavské náměstí (Wenceslas Square).

Václavské náměstí.

The best feature of the former castle site of Wenceslas Square is the remains of the Palace of the Přemyslids: 15th-century frescoes and the episcopal residence with original Romanesque features (► 85). There is a museum in the crypt of dóm sv Václava (Cathedral of St Wenceslas).

The astronomical clock of Olomouc honours Communist teaching

Back to Horní náměstí.

Follow busy 1st May Street. On náměstí Republiky there is the Triton fountain and, on the corner of Hanáckého pluku, the Music Theatre-cum-Olomouc Museum. In Pekařská you pass the Gothic chrám sv Mořice (Church of St Maurice), housing the largest church organ in Moravia. Next to it is an ugly 1970s department store. Turn left and you are back in Upper Square.

Below: *a traditional house in Štramberk*

ŠTRAMBERK ✪✪

What you can see in the open-air museum in Rožnov (▶ 87) is living reality in Štrambek. People live in traditional low Wallachian houses made of rough timber and the whole village smells of wood. There is an **Archeological Museum** by the village square, exhibiting archeological finds from the Šipka caves and Wallachian furniture.

A nearby hill is crowned with a ruined castle. You can climb 166 steps to the top of the fortification to look out over Wallachia.

✚ 31F2
ℹ Náměstí 9
☎ 852240
🚌 Náměstí

Archeological Museum
✉ Náměstí
🕐 Apr–Oct, Tue–Sun 9–12, 1–5
💰 Cheap

31E2
Lazenska 240
☎ 394202
🚉 Nádražní
🚉 Nádražní

Žerotín chateau
☎ 235380
🕐 May–Sep, Tue–Sun 8–12,
1–5; Apr, Oct, Sat–Sun
8–12, 1–4
💰 Cheap

*The arcades are the
most striking feature of
the fine Renaissance
Žerotín chateau*

VELKÉ LOSINY

This pleasant small health resort is surrounded by mountains and forests that are still home to bears. Velké Losiny is a peaceful place and its sole industry of importance is the only paper mill in the Czech Republic producing handmade paper.

Velké Losiny contains one of the best-preserved gems of Renaissance architecture, the U-plan **Žerotín chateau**; an arcaded courtyard has another two storeys of arcades above it, plus a beautiful park. From 1500 to 1800 this beautiful property was occupied by the notorious Žerotín family, whose likenesses hang in the portrait gallery of the castle.

The Žerotíns owe their notoriety to the bloody witch-hunts that they unleashed in 1678. Rumours of vampires were disturbing the peace of the neighbourhood. Witches and devils were supposed to be celebrating satanic rites at Petrovy kameny (Peter's Stone) in the mountains and pursuing their victims from there. Over the next 15 years hundreds of so-called witches were burnt at the stake after secret trials in the Hall of Justice in the chateau.

But most tourists do not come to the town because of its social history or culture but for walking in summer and long-distance skiing in the winter. Hruby (rough) Jesiniky is one of the most attractive areas in the Czech Republic for both. Favourite targets for walkers are Petrovy kameny and the highest point of the mountain, the 1,491m-high Praděd.

Where To...

Above: *the beautiful art-nouveau interior of the café in the Obecni Dům in Prague*

Below: *Moravian costume*

91

Prague

Prices
Prices are approximate, based on a three-course meal for one without drinks and service:

£££ = over 600Kč
££ = 300Kč–600 Kč
£ = under 300Kč

Restaurants

Ambiente (££)
A colourful, somewhat overrated restaurant with American cuisine. Large portions of steaks and chicken legs with spinach and fried potatoes.
✉ Mánesova 59, Praha 2
☎ 6275913
🚇 Jiřího z Poděbrad

Archiv (£££)
French restaurant with local emphasis. Recommended: duck salad with chestnuts, baked shark, beef ragout à la mode.
✉ Masna 3, Praha 1
☎ 24819297
🚇 Náměstí Republiky

Barock Bar & Café (£££)
Restaurant with Asian cuisine. Thai, Japanese, Korean and Chinese dishes.
✉ Pařízská 24, Praha 1
☎ 2329221 🚇 Staroměstská

Break Café (££)
Pleasant café with good service. Gourmet dinners in the evening. Recommended: salad Napoleon, salmon quiche and pasta.
✉ Štepanská 32, Praha 1
☎ 22231065 🚇 Muzeum

Caffé-Ristorante Italia (££)
Modern restaurant close to the citadel. Recommended: lasagne, four-cheese pasta.
✉ Nerudova 17, Praha 1
☎ 530386 🚊 22

Caffrey's Irish Bar (£££)
Relaxing atmosphere. Recommended: Irish salmon, lamb casserole, plaice in wine sauce.
✉ Staroměstské náměstí 10, Praha 1 ☎ 24828031
🚇 Staroměstská

Cerberus (££)
Attractive modern restaurant, popular with locals. Czech cuisine. Recommended: game dishes.
✉ Soukenická 19, Praha 1
☎ 2310985
🚇 Náměstí Republiky

Čínské restaurace (££)
One of the best Chinese restaurants. Good service. Try the Szechuan duck.
✉ Vinohradská 48, Praha 2
☎ 24247549
🚇 Náměstí Míru

Dolly Bell (££)
Balkan restaurant with excellent service. Recommended: burek (meat pasties) and kebabs.
✉ Neklanova 20, Praha 2
☎ 298815 🚇 Vyšehrad

Don Giovanni (££)
Excellent Italian restaurant with first-class service. View of the citadel. Recommended: risotto with wild mushrooms, fresh fish.
✉ Karoliny světlé 34, Praha 1
☎ 265406 🚊 17, 18

Dynamo (££)
Modern restaurant with stylish clientele. Recommended: liver with fried onions, marinated tongue with black sauce.
✉ Pštrossova 29, Praha 1
☎ 294224 🚇 Karlovo náměstí

Fromin (££)
A remarkable establishment and a beautiful view. Czech and French cuisine.
✉ Václavske náměstí 21, Praha 1 ☎ 24232319
🚇 Můstek

Gany's (£)
Simple restaurant. Here Franz Kafka first met Max Brod

responsible for the post-humous fame of his friend.
- ✉ **Národní 20, Praha 1**
- ☎ 297223 🚇 **Národní**

Govinda (££)
Self-service vegetarian restaurant. Ingredients from own farm. Serves Indian dishes.
- ✉ **Soukenická 27, Praha 1**
- ☎ 248216016
- 🚇 **Náměstí Republiky**

Hanavsky Pavilon (£££)
Expensive restaurant in a small but splendid art nouveau building with a wide view over the city.
- ✉ **Letenská sady, Praha 6**
- ☎ 325792 🚇 **Malostranská**

King Solomon (£££)
Kosher restaurant in the Josefov quarter. Recommended: gefilte fish, chicken soup, poached carp with prunes.
- ✉ **Široká 8, Praha 1**
- ☎ 24818752 🚇 **Staroměstská**

La Cambusa (£££)
A good restaurant specialising in fresh fish. Recommended: lobster, trout and carp.
- ✉ **Klicperova, Praha 5**
- ☎ 541533 🚇 **Anděl**

La Provence (£££)
Popular French restaurant with good cuisine and attentive service. Recommended: cassoulet, coq au vin and salads.
- ✉ **Štuparská 9, Praha 1**
- ☎ 2324801
- 🚇 **Náměstí Republiky**

Le Bistrot de Marlène (£££)
Informal but excellent bistro with French cuisine. Limited menu but all dishes are freshly prepared and of good quality.

- ✉ **Plavecká 4, Praha 2**
- ☎ 291077
- 🚌 7, 18, 24

Magdaleny Dobromily Rettigové (££)
This restaurant, named after the 'matriarch of Czech cuisine' (► 95), serves traditional Czech dishes.
- ✉ **Truhlářská 4, Praha 1**
- ☎ 2314483
- 🚇 **Náměstí Republiky**

Malostranská Beseda (££)
Café-restaurant in the former Town Hall of the Lesser Quarter. Reasonable menu of Czech and international cuisine.
- ✉ **Malostranské náměstí, Praha 1** ☎ 535528
- 🚌 12, 27, 57

Myslivna (££)
Game restaurant with a peaceful atmosphere. Wild boar, venison and game excellently prepared, as are the large salads.
- ✉ **Jagellonská, Praha 3**
- ☎ 6270209
- 🚇 **Jiřího z Poděbrad**

Na Vyšehrad (£)
This restaurant with its good Czech cuisine stands on the Vyšehrad Hill opposite the Church of SS Peter and Paul.
- ✉ **K Rotunde 2, Praha 2**
- ☎ 24239297
- 🚇 **Vyšehrad**

Pálffy Palác (£££)
Elegant restaurant in a 17th-century baroque palace on the citadel. Recommended: chicken stuffed with goat's cheese, pork in brandy sauce.
- ✉ **Valštejnská 4, Praha 1**
- ☎ 57320570
- 🚇 **Malostranská**

International
Since the democratic revolution of 1990 the culinary palette of Prague has become multi-coloured. People no longer have just heavy Czech dishes set before them. In addition to Czech cuisine, international cuisine (French, American, Japanese, Chinese and Latin American) has found a permanent place, with Italian restaurants in a prominent position.

Booking Tables

In Prague it is advisable to book a table if you want to eat at a more expensive restaurant. In the cheaper eating places, beer halls and wine bars you can usually find a table to share with other guests.

Pizzeria Kmotra (£)

Very popular, so there is often a queue for tables.

✉ V Jirchářích 2, Praha 1
☎ 24915809   🚋 6, 9, 18, 22

Radost FX Café (£)

Vegetarian restaurant, very popular with young people. Open well into the night.

✉ Belehradská 120, Praha 2
☎ 24254776   Ⓜ I.P. Pavlová

Saté Grill (£)

Small, unpretentious Indonesian restaurant. Recommended: chicken and meat dishes. Good place for lunch after visit to the citadel.

✉ Pohořelec 3, Praha 1
☎ 532133   🚋 22

U Kalicha (£££)

Famous address thanks to the novel *The Good Soldier Schweik* by Jaroslav Hašek. Very touristy.

✉ Na Bojišti 12, Praha 2
☎ 290701   Ⓜ I.P. Pavolová

U Maltézských Rytírů (££)

A peaceful restaurant in the Lesser Quarter. Excellent Czech cuisine. Recommended: game dishes.

✉ Prokopská 10, Praha 1
☎ 536357   🚋 12, 27

V Zátiší (££)

Highly-regarded restaurant with cosy atmosphere. Vegetarian dishes. Good service.

✉ Liliová, Praha 1
☎ 24228977   🚋 17, 18

Železně Dveře (££)

Restaurant with Czech cuisine in a former wine cellar right by the Old Town Square. Excellent Moravian wines.

✉ Michalská 19, Praha 1
☎ 24230841   Ⓜ Můstek

Cafés and bars

Café Milena (£)

Named after Milena Jesenská a friend of Franz Kafka. In the Franz Kafka Centre.

✉ Staroměstské náměstí 22, Praha 1   ☎ 260843
Ⓜ Můstek

Café Montmartre (£)

In the first half of the last century this was the most famous, legendary café cabaret in Prague, a meeting place for the Bohemian set. Open after long-term restoration.

✉ Řetězová 7, Praha 1
Ⓜ Staroměstská

Café de Paris (££)

Art nouveau café in Hotel Paříž. Jazz on Thursdays.

✉ U obecního domu 1, Praha 1
☎ 24222151
Ⓜ Náměstí Republiky

Café Savoy (££)

On an island in the Vltava with high, decorated ceiling, striking chandeliers and a tinkling fountain.

✉ Vitězná 5, Praha 5
☎ 535000   🚋 6, 9, 22

Česká hospoda (£)

A plain café with an eatery at one end. A plaque in the café recalls that in 1911 and 1912 Franz Kafka was a frequent visitor because he became friendly with a Jewish theatre company that met in the present-day dining room.

✉ Vězeňská 9, Praha 1
☎ 2317330
🚋 17   Ⓜ Staroměstská

Ebell kavárna (£)

Excellent coffee in the heart of the Old Town.

✉ Týnská 2, Praha 1
☎ 24895788   Ⓜ Staroměstská

Grand Hotel Europa (££)
The most beautiful building on Wenceslas Square: lovely art nouveau interior. Very touristy.
Václavské náměstí 25
24228117
Můstek

Jazz Café 14 (£)
Young clientele, excellent coffee, cheap beer and jazz from loudspeakers.
Opatovická 14, Praha 1
Národní

Kavárna Obecní Dům (££)
The coffee house in the most attractive art nouveau building in Prague. Meeting place for tourists and business people.
Náměstí Republiky 5
22002763
Náměstí Republiky

Malostranská kavárna (£)
Very old café with two rooms. Restful meeting place for politicians and artists.
Malostranské náměstí 5, Praha 1   533092
12, 27

Pivnice U Černého vola (£)
Café on the citadel where the beer is cheap and the hot snacks are not to be sneezed at.
Loretánské náměstí
22

Pivnice U sv Tomáše (££)
Café in a former brewery next to the Church of St Thomas, also serving vegetarian meals.
Letenská 2   2536776
12, 22   Malostranská

Slávia (£)
The most famous literary coffee house with a lovely view of the citadel and the Petřín. The owner's creed: this *kavárna* must be affordable for students and old ladies.
Smetanova nábřeží 25
24218493   6, 9, 22

The Globe Café and Bookstore (£)
American bookshop cum very 'Bohemian' café. First-class coffee and typical American cookies.
Janovského 14, Praha 7
66712610   Holešovice

U Fleků (£)
Oldest brewery café in Prague, with a garden. Speciality own-brew dark brown beer. Touristy.
Křemencova 11
24915118
Karlovo náměstí

U Kocoura (£)
A very popular café that prides itself on serving the best Plzeňska Prazdroj. Often packed at lunchtime when hot meals are being served.
Nerudova 2   12, 22

U Zlatého tygra (£)
Old café with a lot of regular customers. Became famous through the most popular modern Czech writer Bohumil Hrabal (1914–97, ► 14) who immortalised this café in many of his stories.
Husova 7, Praha 1
24229020   6, 8, 9, 22

Vinárna U Golema (£)
A wine bar in the heart of the old Jewish quarter. In front of the café there is a mosaic of the legendary Golem set in the pavement.
Maislova 8   2328165
Staroměstská

Tradition
In the 19th and early 20th centuries Czech cooks were very popular in Central Europe. They worked in large numbers in the kitchens of the nobility and aristocracy particularly in the Austrian empire. Their bible was the cookbook by Magdalena Rettigové (► 93). The teacher, born in 1806 in Litomyšl, wrote this standard work because she intended to make a contribution to the emancipation of Czech women, which then went hand in hand with the rebirth of Czech national awareness.

North and East Bohemia

Pork Festival
Pork is the most popular ingredient in the Czech kitchen. It is not therefore surprising that the slaughter of pigs (*zabijačka*) each autumn is a celebration, especially in the countryside. Anyone who can afford it buys a fat pig that is almost ritually slaughtered in the presence of friends and relations. Perishable parts are eaten straight away, for example the blood is made into a soup, which is on the menu in many restaurants in November. Don't have a fit: if you like black pudding you will like this soup.

Restaurants

Děčín
Zámecká vinárna (£)
Restaurant with good cuisine and obliging service. The Czech dishes can certainly be recommended.
✉ U brány 21
☎ 24750

Hradec Králové
Černý kůň (£)
Beer bar-cum-restaurant which serves meals of reasonable quality.
✉ Malé náměstí 10
☎ 5592427

Hospoda pod věží (£)
Quiet restaurant. Serves good, traditional Czech dishes.
✉ Velké náměstí 36
☎ 5615032

Pivnice Na hradě (£)
A plain but certainly not unfriendly beer bar where plain Czech meals are served.
✉ Tomkova

Jičín
Restaurace Albrecht (£)
Peaceful restaurant with highly-recommended Czech dishes.
✉ Husova 39
☎ 21403

Vinárna U Anděla (£)
A wine house in the central square that serves good meals.
✉ Valdšyejnovo náměstí

Karlštejn
U Janů (£)
Simple restaurant in centre of the village. Typical Czech menu.
✉ Náměstí 10 ☎ Telephone reservations not accepted

U královny Dagmar (£)
'At King Dagmar' is a bed-and-breakfast establishment where the restaurant is open for passers-by who are not staying the night. The food is first class.
✉ Podzámek
☎ 684614

Konopiště
Hotel-restaurant Myslivna (££)
The restaurant is in a luxurious chalet. Speciality: game dishes.
✉ Podzámek
☎ 22469

Pošta (£)
This hotel in the nearby Benešov serves plain but well-prepared meals in its restaurant.
✉ Tyršova 162
☎ 22355

Kutná Hora
Havířský Šenk (££)
Restaurant in a wine cellar, where there is dancing to music during meals.
✉ Šultysova 154
☎ 53997

U Anděla (£)
This is a pleasant beer bar but food is also available served by obliging staff.
✉ Václavské náměstí 8

U tří pávů (£)
A café-cum-restaurant with a garden terrace which is very pleasant in the summer.
✉ Palackého náměstí 379
☎ 50322

Čínská restaurace (£)
Very good Chinese restaurant with a restful atmosphere.
✉ Náměstí Národního odboje 48 ☎ 514151

Litoměřice
Radniční sklípek (£)
The restaurant occupies a former wine cellar. The Czech dishes are reliable.
- ✉ Mírové náměstí 21
- ☎ 6626

Hotel-restaurant Helena (££)
On the route from Litoměřice to Terezín and Prague. Reasonable international cuisine.
- ✉ Želetická 10
- ☎ 5179

Vinárna Bašta (£)
This wine bar occupies a former bastion. The Czech cuisine is good.
- ✉ Pokratická 91

Litomysl
Dalibor (££)
Quiet restaurant that is part of a hotel outside the centre. Good regional cuisine.
- ✉ Kamenského 1053
- ☎ 618584

Zlatá Hvězda (££)
Hotel-restaurant right in the centre of the town. International cuisine with good service.
- ✉ Smetanovo náměstí 84
- ☎ 615338

Mělník
Stará škola (S)
This wine bar behind the church serves good meals. There is a beautiful view from the tables by the window.
- ✉ Škola 3

U soutoku (££)
Restaurant on the ground floor of the castle, lovely view and very good food.
- ✉ Zámek ☎ Telephone reservations not accepted

U Tomáše (£)
This friendly restaurant close to the castle has a varied Czech menu and excellent wines.
- ✉ Svatováclavská 15
- ☎ 627357

Spindlerův Mlýn
Hotel-restaurant Panorama (£)
A plain hotel with an equally plain cuisine which is reflected in the price.
- ✉ Svatý Petr 136
- ☎ 93352

U Petra (£)
Small restaurant in friendly pension. Good cooking.
- ✉ Svaty Petr 200
- ☎ Telephone reservations not accepted

Svitavy
Schindlerův haj (£)
This is a quiet restaurant in a family hotel with good international and regional cuisine.
- ✉ Pražská 24 ☎ 22395

Terezín
Parkhotel (£)
Hotel-restaurant with international cuisine.
- ✉ Machová 162 ☎ 92260

Turnov
U sv Jana (£)
This restaurant on the first floor of the pension of the same name is the best in town.
- ✉ Hluboká 142 ☎ 23325

Žatec
Hotel-restaurant Hop (££)
A restaurant with both international and traditional Czech cuisine. Also beer and a wine bar.
- ✉ Bratťt Čapku 2705
- ☎ 43801

Coffee
Traditionally a lot of coffee has been drunk in Central Europe. The coffee house was indeed a centre of culture where artists and intellectuals met to discuss or to read the newspapers. In Czech towns there are still many of these *kavárnas* where you can usually also have snacks. Although filter coffee and espresso can be found everywhere these days, the average Czech still drinks *turecká* (Turkish): ground coffee over which boiling water is poured.

West and South Bohemia

Drinking Water

Because Czech tap water is often unpalatable many Czechs prefer to drink mineral water. It is available everywhere and is fairly cheap. Each of the health resorts produces one or more of its own brands. The most popular sparkling *minerální* is Mattoni (from Karlovy Vary); the most popular still water is Dobrá voda (literally 'good water' but named after the South Bohemian place of origin).

Restaurants

České Budějovice
U Hrušků (££)
Large restaurant, also suitable for groups. Quality of cuisine is reasonable to good.
✉ Česká 23 ☎ 35670

Restaurant Zvon (£££)
The restaurant of Hotel Zvon in the main square is excellent. International and regional cuisine.
✉ Přemysla Ottokara II náměstí ☎ 7311383

Český Krumlov
Cikánská jizba (£)
This friendly, sometimes noisy gypsy eating place is run by a Roma family who serve excellent goulash dishes.
✉ Dlouhá 31

Krčma Markéta (££)
A café-restaurant near the castle, where music and staff in historic costumes imitate a medieval and Renaissance atmosphere.
✉ Latrán 67 ☎ 3829

Jelenka (££)
Historic restaurant with traditional Czech cuisine.
✉ Jelení zahrada ☎ 4628

Cheb
Staročeská restaurace (£)
One of the best restaurants in the town, serving Czech, international and Chinese dishes.
✉ Kamenná 1 ☎ 422170

Restaurant Hvězda (£)
This restaurant is part of the Hotel Hvězda at the end of the main square.
✉ Náměstí Jiřího z Poděbrad ☎ 422549

Domažlice
Singapore (£)
This café-restaurant with its exotic name in fact serves first-class Czech and western European dishes.
✉ Kostelní 12 ☎ 725783

Hluboká
Restaurace Eleonora (£)
Between the village and the castle. Rather touristy but reasonable food.
✉ Masarykovo 421

Jindřichův Hradec
U zlata husa (£)
Restaurant of Hotel Concertino. Good regional cuisine, pleasant service.
✉ Náměstí Míru 41 ☎ 362320

Karlovy Vary
Promenáda (££)
Busy restaurant popular with the locals. The relatively high prices are not unusual because everything is expensive in this health resort.
✉ Tříště 31 ☎ 25648

Zámecká restaurace Karel IV (££)
Good restaurant in old castle gatehouse near the Market Colonnade. International and regional dishes.
✉ Lázeňská 146 ☎ 3227255

Restaurant Pupp (£££)
If you want to enjoy the elegant atmosphere and former glory of this historic kingdom and the still fashionable Grand Hotel, you will have to pay handsomely for the extensive and excellent menu.
✉ Mírové náměstí 2 ☎ 3109111

Klatovy
U hejtmana (£)
Grill room where standard traditional Czech dishes are available.
✉ Balbínová
☎ 20650

Mariánské Lázně
Jalta (£)
This is a very reasonably priced *restaurace* in a generally very expensive health resort.
✉ Hlavní 43
☎ Telephone reservations not accepted

Restaurace Classic (£)
First-class restaurant, given the low prices. Also serves a selection of vegetarian dishes.
✉ Hlavní 125
☎ 622807

Hotel-restaurant Český Dvůr (£)
Plain restaurant with reasonable cuisine. Pleasant ambience.
✉ Žavísin 35
☎ 622490

Písek
Hotel-restaurant Bíla růže (££)
Very good place to eat, with international cuisine and obliging staff.
✉ Šrámkova 169
☎ 214931

Plzeň
Pivnice U Salzmannů (£)
A beer hall that is a household name in Plzeň. Serves very good Czech cuisine.
✉ Pražská 8
☎ 7235484

Vinárna Zlatý hrozen (£)
A wine cellar where you can also have reasonable and cheap meals.
✉ Bezručova 36
☎ Telephone reservations not accepted

Prachatice
Královská (£)
Cosy restaurant specialising in South Bohemian dishes.
✉ Husova 106
☎ 322952

Příbram
Modry Hrozen (£)
A plain-looking hotel, but serves good regional food.
✉ Náměstí T.G. Masaryk 143
☎ 28007

Sušice
Na Růžku (£)
This restaurant, which is situated in the centre, specialises in regional cuisine.
✉ Dlouhá ves 152
☎ 526130

Tábor
Restaurace Apetit (£)
A large beer bar where you can also eat on a pleasant terrace.
✉ Náměstí Křižíka 1878
☎ Telephone reservations not accepted

Třeboň
Bílý Koníček (£)
The place to go if you want to eat excellent carp (or other freshwater fish) in this carp-rearing centre.
✉ Masarykovo náměstí 48

Restaurace Beseda (£)
A plain restaurant, reached through the Town Hall, especially popular with the locals.
✉ Masarykovo náměstí 2
☎ 3323

Bad Name Lingers
Czech cuisine has the former Communist authorities to thank for its bad name. They believed that food had simply to be nourishing and in their meddling way they laid down detailed rules for restaurant food. In every restaurant the dishes had to conform to the same directives as regards quantity and ingredients, so that outside the home only uniform national dishes were served. There are still some restaurants where these directives, enshrined in two thick volumes, remain alive and well.

South Moravia

Jídelna
Apart from restaurants, snack bars and beer and wine bars it is also possible to satisfy your hunger in a special eating area at the butcher's. In a *jidelna*, where you usually have to stand at a counter, you can enjoy meat dishes, goulash or main-course soup prepared on the premises with bread and a garnish, at very little cost.

Brno
Moravska Chalupa (££)
An outstanding wine bar with very reasonable cuisine.
✉ Křižkovského 47
☎ 43143100

Pivnice Zemský dům (£)
Small, cosy salad bar, very popular with vegetarians.
✉ Kounicova 1
☎ 43211669

U Schodů (£)
Traditional and locally popular restaurant with a very attractive cuisine and good service.
✉ Pekařská 29
☎ 43211518

Jihlava
Grand (£)
This hotel-restaurant is very popular with local people and visitors because of its good food at fair prices.
✉ Husova 3   ☎ 23541

Kroměříž
Radniční sklípek (££)
A small but excellent cellar restaurant. Czech and international cuisine.
✉ Kovářská 4   ☎ Telephone reservations not accepted

Morava (£)
Plain but good dishes, including Moravian specialities.
✉ Kovářská 13
☎ 334775

Lednice-Valtice
Hotel-restaurant Hubertus (££)
This restaurant is housed in the castle of Valtice. Serves good regional and international cuisine with excellent wines.
✉ Náměstí Svobody
☎ 94537

Luhačovice
Alexandria (££)
Elegant restaurant in an even more elegant hotel. Very good cooking.
✉ Masarykova 567
☎ 932750

Mikulov
U Priaristů (££)
Modern café-restaurant with good cuisine and excellent wines. Access through Pension Prima.
✉ Priaristů 8   ☎ 3793

Moravský Krumlov
Hotel Jednota (£)
Excellent restaurant in a simple hotel.
✉ T.G. Masaryka 27
☎ 322373

Slavkov
Sokolský dům (£)
The best restaurant in this touristy town, and at the best prices.
✉ Palackého náměstí 75
☎ 4221103

Telč
Pod věží (£)
A restaurant serving Moravian specialities that diners can enjoy in a sunny garden.
✉ Palackého 26   ☎ 7243889

Zlín
Garni Zlín (££)
This hotel has the best restaurant in a town that is not conspicuous in the gastronomic field.
✉ Náměstí T.G. Masaryk 1335
☎ 7211941

Znojmo
Restaurace Morava (££)
A restaurant that specialises in regional recipes but also serves international dishes.
✉ Horní náměstí 17

North Moravia

Frýdek Mistek
Delta (£)
Plain restaurant in the centre with reliable food.
✉ J.V. Sládka
☎ Telephone reservations not accepted

Šněhurka (£)
This restaurant specialises in Moravian dishes and game.
✉ U staré pošty
☎ Telephone reservations not accepted

Hranice
Na myslivné (££)
Restaurant that, as its name ('Hunting Lodge') implies, specialises in game dishes.
✉ Třída 1. máje 67
☎ 201289

Na Hradbách (£)
Traditional restaurant in the historic town square.
✉ Masarykovo náměstí 39
☎ 202252

Kopřivnice
Tatrarest (£)
This restaurant belongs to the Tatra Hotel a few houses away. Reliable cuisine with friendly service.
✉ Záhumenní 1151
☎ 813101

Olomouc
Mikulovská vinárna (£)
This is a wine bar that also serves good food, and naturally, excellent Moravian wine.
✉ 28. října 107
☎ 5220354

Centrum bufet (£)
An excellent place for hot and cold lunches. This cafeteria closes at 5PM.
✉ Třída 1. máje 23
☎ Telephone reservations not accepted

Neptun (££)
Very popular because of its delicious fish dishes.
✉ Komenského 5
☎ 5389349

Drápal (££)
Busy restaurant. Vegetarian dishes as well as international cuisine.
✉ Havlíčkova 50
☎ 5225818

Opava
U bílého koníčka (£)
'At the White Horse' is a particularly friendly restaurant serving international cuisine.
✉ Dolní náměstí 14
☎ 212904

Ostrava
Pivnice Radegast (£)
A beer bar with a wide choice of regional dishes and reasonably-priced menus of the day.
✉ 28. října
☎ Telephone reservations not accepted

Rožnov
Majerův dvůr (£)
Popular restaurant in a courtyard. Fish as well as meat on the menu.
✉ Nerudova 141
☎ 53158

Štramberk
Sipka (£)
This restaurant, attached to the hotel of the same name, serves good food.
✉ Náměstí 37   ☎ 852181

Velké Losiny
Zerotín (£)
Good cuisine, including vegetarian dishes, in the hotel of the same name.
✉ Rude armády 333
☎ 248307

McBůček
Even in the Czech Republic it is impossible to avoid McDonald's. The Communists had hardly taken to their heels when the American fast-food chain appeared in the marketplace. It was not an immediate success: given the low wages in the Czech Republic, the uniform restaurants were in the more expensive category. In addition, what was on offer was not really to Czech taste. Not, that is, until the McDonald's board allowed the Czech managers to develop the McBůček: a roll filled with lean pork.

Prague

Prices
Prices are approximate, per room per night.

£££ = over 3,000Kč
££ = 1,500–3,000Kč
£ = under 1,500Kč

Savoy (£££)
A modern and luxurious hotel on the northern approach to the citadel complex. Very popular with politicians, diplomats and film stars.
✉ **Keplerova 6** ☎ **24302430**
🚌 **8, 22**

U Kříže (££)
Small, modern hotel in busy main street of the Lesser Quarter.
✉ **Újezd 25** ☎ **533326**
🚌 **12, 22**

Hotel Hoffmeister (£££)
One of the pleasantest hotels in the Lesser Quarter at the foot of the citadel. The owner is the son of the best known pre-war caricaturist, much of whose work hangs on the walls.
✉ **Pod bruskou 9** ☎ **5618155**
🚌 **18, 22** Ⓜ **Malostranská**

Unitas Pension – La Prison (£)
This former convent in the city centre once housed the Communist secret service: Václav Havel was held in Cell 6. This and others have been converted into simple rooms.
✉ **Bartolomějska 9**
☎ **2327700** Ⓜ **Můstek**

Central (££)
Traditional hotel in a quiet, central street of the Old Town. Reasonable restaurant.
✉ **Rybná 8** ☎ **248127**
Ⓜ **Republiky náměstí**

Ungelt (£££)
This centuries-old hotel has been much modernised and stands in a quiet side street of Staroměstská náměstí, behind the Týn cathedral.
✉ **Štupartská** ☎ **2481330**
Ⓜ **Můstek**

Hotel Albatros (££)
This is a converted ship moored in the River Vltava near the centre. Prices are halved out of season.
✉ **Ňábřeží Ludvíka Svobody**
☎ **24810541** 🚌 **3**

Harmony (£££)
An attractive, relatively small hotel with large, pleasant double rooms. Atmospheric restaurant.
✉ **Na poříčí 31**
☎ **232000** 🚌 **14, 24, 26**
Ⓜ **Republiky náměstí**

Palac (£££)
Old but modernised art nouveau hotel a stone's throw from the Václavské náměstí. Popular with business people.
✉ **Panská 1** ☎ **24093111**
🚌 **3, 9, 24** Ⓜ **Můstek**

Zlatá Husa (£££)
A celebrated old hotel that appears in Kafka's novel *America*. Many Czech business people stay here.
✉ **Václavské náměstí 5**
☎ **24193111** Ⓜ **Můstek**

Pension-hotel City (£)
Quiet hotel in a side street in the busy Vinohrady district.
✉ **Belgická 10** ☎ **6911334**
🚌 **6, 11, 22** Ⓜ **Náměstí Miru**

Union (££)
A beautifully restored hotel at the foot of the Vyšerad. Excellent restaurant.
✉ **Ostrčilovo náměstí 4**
☎ **6927506** 🚌 **7, 24**

Belverder (££)
A tall, old hotel on the northern access to the citadel, the traffic artery of the Holešovice district. Halfway between the main market and the Sparta football stadium.

✉ **Milady Horákove 19**
☎ 374741 🚇 1, 8, 25, 26
🚇 Vltavská

Mövenpick hotel (£££)

Modern purpose-built hotel in the Smichov district. Very popular with tour groups. Next to where Mozart lodged in the Villa Bertamka.
✉ **Mozartova 261/1**
☎ 57151111 🚇 4, 16
🚇 Anděl

Don Giovanni (£££)

A very fashionable modern hotel, which at the weekend hosts artistic performances. Otherwise a typical business hotel outside the city centre but easy to reach from there.
✉ **Vinohradská 157** ☎ 670316
🚇 11, 16, 26 🚇 Želivského

Bilý Lev (££)

The 'White Lion' is just outside the centre in the Nusle district. The great benefit is the price/service ratio.
✉ **Cimbukova 20, Praha 3**
☎ 271126 🚇 5, 9, 26

Hostel Sokol (£)

This cheap hostel is well situated in the Lesser Quarter, just by the Charles Bridge. Usually busy in the summer.
✉ **Hellichova 1, Praha 1**
☎ 9971691 🚇 12, 27

Bilá Labut (££)

Hotel on the edge of the Old Town. Rooms have TV. There is a bar and restaurant.
✉ **Biskupská 9, Praha 1**
☎ 2324540 🚇 Florenc

Hotel Europa (££)

This very attractive, well-situated and very popular hotel, on account of its *kavárna*, is cheaper than you would imagine.

✉ **Václavské náměstí 25**
☎ 24228117 🚇 Můstek

Hotel Pariž (£££)

This is one of the best 'old' hotels in Prague: a neo-Gothic building with a lovely art nouveau interior.
✉ **U Obecniho domu 1, Praha 1**
☎ 24222151 🚇 Republiky

Kampa (££)

This modernised hotel in a 17th-century building is centrally situated in the Lesser Quarter and is popular with group travellers.
✉ **Všehradová 16, Praha 1**
☎ 24510409 🚇 12, 22

Větrník (££)

This pension has been establised in an old windmill in the western suburb of Břevnov. There is a tennis court for sports enthusiasts.
✉ **U Větrníku 40, Praha 6**
☎ 3519622 🚇 1, 2, 18

Řepy (£)

The hotel lies in a suburb of the same name. Reasonable facilities: showers in all rooms, restaurant and terrace.
✉ **Makovského 1177, Praha 6**
☎ 3014891 🚇 4, 7, 9

U Krále Jiřího (£)

A popular, somewhat noisy place in the Old Town with its own bar and restaurant. All rooms have shower, telephone and TV.
✉ **Liliová 10, Praha 1**
☎ 24222013 🚇 Sraromětská

U Tří Pštrosů (£££)

Extremely attractive 17th-century hotel at the foot of the Charles Bridge. Its restaurant is well regarded.
✉ **Dražického náměstí 12, Praha 1** ☎ 24510779
🚇 Malostranská

Hotel Reservations

The Czech Republic, which not long ago was a relatively inaccessible country, has seen a huge increase in tourists over the last decade or so. The hotel industry has not been able to keep up with the demand. It is therefore advisable at peak seasons (May–September, Easter and Christmas) to book accommodation in advance in the main tourist centres: Prague, Česky Krumlov, Brno and the Krkonoše.

North and East Bohemia

Price Differences
During the Communist era tourists were obliged to stay in certain hotels whereas nowadays they are free to stay where they want. It does, however, happen that Czech citizens pay less for hotel rooms than foreigners. The reason given is that the average income in the Czech Republic is considerably lower than elsewhere in Europe.

Děčín
Česká koruna (££)
This very reasonable hotel stands in the centre of the town and has single and double rooms. Breakfast is included.
✉ **Masarykovo náměstí 60**
☎ **22093**

Hradec Králové
U sv Lukáše (£)
A luxurious pension right in the centre of the town. The reasonable price per night includes breakfast.
✉ **Úzká 208**
☎ **5210616**

Černigov (££)
The hotel is situated opposite the railway station. It has a restaurant and bar. Breakfast is included.
✉ **Riegerovo náměstí 1494**
☎ **5814111**

Jičín
Rieger (£)
This pension provides some of the luxury rare in reasonably cheap accommodation. It is just outside the centre.
✉ **Náměstí Komenského**
☎ **25480**

Kutná Hora
U Vlašského Dvora (£)
One of the best hotels. It is in the town centre, and has a sauna as well as a good restaurant.
✉ **28. října 511**
☎ **4618**

U Rytířů (£)
In this friendly hostel you can hear the centuries-old stone fountain, which stands just outside the entrance. Mainly double rooms with showers.
✉ **Rejskovo náměstí 123**
☎ **2256**

Litoměřice
Salva Guarda (£)
This hotel occupies a Renaissance building the 'Black Eagle' in the centre. Nicely furnished rooms.
✉ **Mírove náměstí 12**
☎ **3296**

Litomyšl
Zlatá Hvězda (£)
Traditional hotel in the main square with good restaurant. Fully-equipped rooms including TV.
✉ **Smetanovo náměstí 84**
☎ **615338**

Mělník
Ludmila
For motorists this is the most recommended hotel in a village where mainly bed and breakfast is on offer.
✉ **Pražská**   ☎ **622423**

Špindlerův Mlýn
Panorama (£)
Of all the hotels in this winter sports resort this is the one recommended from the point of view of price/quality ratio.
✉ **Svatý Petr 136**   ☎ **93352**

Terezín
Parkhotel (£)
There is little overnight accommodation available in the former ghetto town. This hotel is very plain and accordingly cheap.
✉ **Máchova 162**
☎ **92260**

Turnov
Karel IV (£)
This hotel does not look attractive from outside but once inside everything exceeds expectations. Rooms with shower and WC.
✉ **Žižkova 501**
☎ **23855**

West and South Bohemia

České Budějovice

U Solné Brány (££)
Attractive hotel in the peaceful Diocesan gardens. Rooms with balcony and TV, plus good restaurant.

✉ **Radniční 11**   ☎ **54121**

U Tří lvů (£££)
'The Three Lions' is a couple of minutes from the main square. It has a restaurant, nightclub and fitness centre.

✉ **U tří lvů 3**   ☎ **59900**

Český Krumlov

Hotel Růže (££)
This hotel occupies a Renaissance building with a view of the Vltava. It was formerly a Jesuit hospice.

✉ **Horní 154**   ☎ **711141**

Pension Falko (£)
A plain pension with shower, WC and minibar in all rooms. Some also have TV.

✉ **Rooseveltova 152**   ☎ **4262**

Karlovy Vary

Heluan (££)
A relatively small hotel with restaurant, bar, nightclub and terrace. Some rooms have TV.

✉ **Tržíště 41**   ☎ **25756**

Dvořák (£££)
Everything you expect in an expensive health resort hotel: swimming pool, sauna, sports centre and spa treatments.

✉ **Nová louka 11**   ☎ **24145**

Mariánské Lázně

Helvetia (££)
A mid-class hotel for a reasonable price, given the local tariffs. Modern rooms equipped with TV, shower and WC.

✉ **Hlavni 23**   ☎ **622629**

Martina Pension (£)
This pension rents out small apartments. WC and bathrooms have to be shared with other guests.

✉ **Jiráskova 6**
☎ **623647**

Plzeň

Slovan (£)
A large, comfortable hotel by a park. Has a restaurant and bar.

✉ **Smetanovy sady 1**
☎ **7227256**

Rosso (££)
This modern hotel has small but pleasant rooms with WC, shower and TV. The restaurant serves French cuisine.

✉ **Pallova 12**
☎ **226473**

Prachatice

Zlatá Stezka (£)
The 'Golden Trail' is a romantic old hotel on the Renaissance main square. Double rooms with WC and shower.

✉ **Velké náměstí 50**
☎ **21841**

Tábor

Bohemia (££)
This hotel by the station is one of the best places to stay in Tábor. Rooms with shower and TV. Has a good restaurant.

✉ **Husovo náměstí 591**
☎ **22828**

Třeboň

Zlatá Hvězda (££)
Good hotel in the main square. Here you can visit the local brewery and organise a day's fishing, and there are bicycles for hire.

✉ **Masarykova náměstí 107**
☎ **757111**

Garni
Some hotels include the word *garni* in their name. It means that they do not have a restaurant and only serve a simple breakfast.

House Numbers
Houses and buildings in the Czech Republic have two numbers. The blue number is the one used in addresses. The red one is a survey number used for official purposes only.

South Moravia

Bed and Breakfast
There is plenty of relatively cheap accommodation available in private houses. Particularly in small places, you often see boards with *Zimmer frei* (Room to let). In larger places and cities you can approach the letting agencies, to be found on the railway stations, or in tourist offices such as Čedok, for private rooms.

Brno
Grandhotel Brno (£££)
The best (and most expensive) hotel in Brno, opposite the railway station. Two excellent restaurants, a casino and a nightclub.
✉ Benešova 18–20
☎ 42321287

Slávia (££)
Nice, not very remarkable hotel. Rooms have bath, WC, TV. Good restaurant.
✉ Solniční 15   ☎ 42321249

Pegas (£)
Comfortable, pleasant hotel in a quiet street and yet in the centre. Rooms with bath. Breakfast included.
✉ Jakubská 4   ☎ 42211232

Jihlava
U labutě (£)
A pleasant hotel in the city centre. Rooms with shower and WC. Has a good restaurant.
✉ Náměstí Republiky 70
☎ 22949

Kroměříž
Bouček (££)
This historic town, which is a conservation area, has few hotels of which Bouček is the best. It has recently been renovated and provides rooms with or without bath.
✉ Velké náměstí 30
☎ 25777

Lilie (£)
This is an excellent pension in the town centre. Rooms are double with shower and WC.
✉ Ztracená 67   ☎ 23871

Mikulov
Roháty krokodýl (£)
Small double rooms without shower and TV and rather expensive, everything considered.
✉ Husova 8   ☎ 2692

Telč
Pod kaštany (£)
Old-fashioned hotel just outside the town. Single and double rooms with bath. Breakfast included.
✉ Štěpnická 409   ☎ 7213042

Na Hrázi (££)
This is a small hotel (15 rooms) but with all facilities. Breakfast is included.
✉ Na hrázi 78
☎ 7213151

Uherské Hradiště
Grand (£)
An excellent hotel in the town centre. Single and double rooms with shower and WC.
✉ Palackého náměstí 349
☎ 551511

Žďár
U labutě (£)
Pleasant hotel on the main square. Single and double rooms with shower and WC.
✉ Náměstí Republiky 70
☎ 22949

Zlín
Interhotel Moskva (££)
The most fashionable hotel in town. Architecturally an example of the functional school. All facilities plus good restaurant.
✉ Náměstí Prďce 2512
☎ 8361111

Znojmo
U Huberta (£)
First class pension with single and double rooms but bathrooms are shared. Own restaurant.
✉ Dolní Česká 38
☎ 70102

North Moravia

Frýdek Místek
Centrum (££)
Reliable hotel near the town centre. Rooms with shower and WC. Has its own restaurant.

✉ **Na poříčí 494**   ☎ **45227**

Hranice
Růžek (£)
This comfortable pension off the main square has only 11 beds, divided among single and double rooms. Breakfast is included.

✉ **Radnicní 33**
☎ **201756**

Hukvaldy
Pod oborou (£)
Quiet pension in the country. Rooms with bath, WC and TV.

✉ **Hukvaldy 42**
☎ **53794**

Kopřivnice
Tatra (£)
The most obvious name for a hotel in the town in which the famous vehicle brand was made. Reasonable double and single rooms and its own restaurant.

✉ **Záhumenní 24**
☎ **321911**

Olomouc
Gemo (££)
A modern hotel. Pleasant rooms, with bath, TV and minibar. Good restaurant, *kavárna* and wine bar.

✉ **Pavelčákova 22**
☎ **5222065**

Národní dům (£)
The rooms in this hotel, which given the price are very acceptable, have a bath or shower. There is a good restaurant.

✉ **8. května 21**
☎ **5224806**

Stavařov (£)
If you do not want to pay much but still have a decent room this is the place to go.

✉ **U mistni dráhy 1**
☎ **5413940**

Opava
Pension Koruna (££)
Apart from the most expensive hotel of this name in the town square, there is also this pension Koruna where the rooms are fully equipped.

✉ **Řatibořska 95**   ☎ **61394**

Ostrava
Polský dům (££)
This is the nicest hotel in the town. It is situated in a somewhat tumbledown, spacious and century-old art nouveau building but has good rooms with WC, bath and TV.

✉ **Poděbradova 53**
☎ **232001**

Rožnov
Evroplan (££)
The best hotel in this touristy place. Single and double rooms with shower, WC and TV.

✉ **Horní Paseky 451**
☎ **55835**

Štramberk
Šipka (£)
You can obtain very cheap, plain rooms in this hotel but there are also more modern, more expensive rooms with shower, WC and TV.

✉ **Náměsti 14**   ☎ **852181**

Velké Losiny
Žerotín (££)
Rather small hotel, but very well equipped. Has its own restaurant.

✉ **Rude Armády 333**
☎ **248307**

Mountain Huts
In the mountain regions – Krkonoše, Beskydy and the Šumava – it is also possible to spend a night in a *chata*, *bouda* or *chalupa* (➤ 114). Some of these mountain huts are extremely basic but others could be called luxurious. The accommodation in the latter category is also referred to as *horský hotelý*: mountain hotels.

Attractions for Children

Playgrounds

The cities and towns of the Czech Republic usually have one or more parks that contain playgrounds. Large hotels and holiday centres often also have mini-golf courses. You can take tram or horse-drawn carriage rides in Prague and České Budějovice. If you are visiting Prague with children, a boat trip on the River Vltava is a good idea.

Prague

Tradiční loutkové divadlo Zvoneček (Puppet Theatre)

The puppet theatre has a long tradition in the Czech Republic and many towns have one. This is one of the most famous in Prague.

🖂 Braníčka 504
☎ 44462826   🚊 3, 16, 17, 21
🕐 All year 5–7PM

Exhibition Ground

There is an old-fashioned funfair on the Výstaviště (Exhibition Ground), where international exhibitions and trade fairs have been held since 1891. The attractions include a musical fountain, a swimming pool, and a planetarium with performances daily 2–5PM.

🖂 U Výstaviště   ☎ 8279204
🚊 5, 12, 17   🚇 Holešovice
🕐 Daily 9–6

Muzeum Hraček (Toy Museum)

A fascinating toy museum close to the citadel. There are puppets, model cars, aeroplanes and trains, tin soldiers and dolls' houses. Some exhibits are more than 150 years old.

🖂 Jiřská 6   ☎ 24371111
🚊 22   🕐 Daily 9:30–5:30.
Closed Mon

Mirror Maze

Bludiště (Mirror Maze) is in Petřín Park opposite the Church of St Lawrence (▶ 33). The labyrinth of mirrors ends in a panoramic view of the battle of Prague at the end of the Thirty Years' War and a room with with distorting mirrors.

🕐 Mar–Oct daily 10–4
🚊 12, 22, then by Újezd cable car (daily 9:30–7:45)

Brno

Technical Museum

This is housed in the former Franciscan monastery. The Panorama, constructed in 1890, depicting the wonders of the world in three dimensions, is very spectacular.

🖂 Františkánská 1
🕐 Tue–Sun 9–12, 1–4

Planetarium

There is an observatory just outside Brno, on Kraví Hora Hill. The planetarium is open to the public.

🖂 Kraví hora   🚊 4
🕐 Daily 9–12, 1–4

Radost divadlo (Puppet Theatre)

Like many Czech towns Brno has its puppet theatre. The Radost, just outside the city, has a national reputation.

🖂 Bratislavská 32
🕐 Sun 10 and 2:30

České Budějovice

Museum of the Horse-Drawn Railway

In the Památky koněspřežní želecnice you can see what the oldest railway line on the continent looked like and how it worked (▶ 50). It is just outside the city, near the campsite.

🖂 Mánesova 10
🕐 Tue–Sun 9:30–12, 12:30–5

Český Krumlov

Masked Ballroom

Maškarní sál on the baroque route through the castle complex has trompe l'œil paintings from 1748 in the former ballroom (▶ 16). The artist Lederer portrayed himself in one corner as an observer drinking coffee.

🖂 See castle (▶ 16)

Old Krumlov
The Regional Museum, which contains a great deal about the history of the Šumava, has a whole room devoted to a model of Česky Krumlov as it was in 1800. Its most remarkable feature is that it is made of pottery.

🔲 Horní 161
🕐 Tue–Fri 9–12, 12:30–4, Sat–Sun 1–4

Jihlava
Zoo
This is one of the most attractive zoos in the Czech Republic, more so than the zoos in Prague or Brno. It houses more than 400 animals, including rare Sumatran tigers and many apes. Both animals and visitors have plenty of space.

🔲 Křížkova
🕐 All year 9–5

Jindřichův Hradec
Bethlehem Nativity Scene
The Regional Museum contains *Betlém*, a model of Bethlehem at the time of the birth of Christ. The 18th-century artist worked on the model, which has about 1000 moving figures, for nearly 60 years (► 52).

Kutná Hora
Ossuary Chapel
At first sight this seems rather gruesome but a closer look reveals it as witty and artistic. The 14th-century All Saints' Chapel in the suburb of Sedlec is completely furnished and decorated with bones and skulls (► 21).

Labské pískovce
Boat Trip
Children find walking in this region (► 28, 42, 113) with its steep cliffs and deep ravines very tiring. The solution is a boat trip on the Kamenice, a tributary of the Labe, that flows through spectacular deep gorges. From just outside Hřensko, on the German border, boats leave every half hour. There is a choice of long or short trips; as far as Jetřichovice, where the Labské piscovce ends in the east, the trip is divided into four stages with three stop and change places.

🕐 May–Sep daily; Apr and Oct Sat–Sun; 35Kč per stage

Liberec
Naïve Theatre
The Naïve Theatre is one of the nicest puppet theatres in the Czech Republic and although it is aimed at children it is also fun for their parents. The programme is changed frequently.

Naivni divadlo
🔲 Moskevská 18
☎ 3677

Polička
Martinů Museum
You do not have to be a connoisseur of modern classical music to visit the birthplace of this inter-nationally famous Czech composer (1890–1959). It is situated high up in the church tower in Polička (► 41) where the family lived because his father was on fire watch. After a steep climb you reach a tiny home furnished as it was when Martinů was a young boy.

🔲 Tyrova 5   🕐 Apr–Oct Tue–Sun 10–12, 1–4, Sun 12–4
♿ None   💰 Moderate

The Tram
A tram ride is the ideal way to introduce children to Prague. Most lines follow long routes which cross the city. The best one is Line 22 which runs from the Skalka district on the southeastern edge of the city to the historic Bílá Hora (White Mountain) with its former summer place, now a museum, on the extreme northwest edge. This route passes through the old historic centre, over the Vltava river, through the Malá Strana and past the citadel. Tram tickets, also valid for the metro, can be bought at metro stations, in tobacconists and at reception in many hotels.

Entertainment

Buying Tickets
It is better to buy tickets for concerts and plays at the relevant theatre or from official agencies. At the latter you will, however, pay a hefty supplement. Tickets are almost always still available at the booking office, from an hour before the start of the performance.

Theatres and Concert Halls

Prague
Convent of St Agnes
Chamber-music concerts are performed regularly in this former convent. It also houses art exhibitions.
✉ U milosrdných 17

Hudební Divadlo Karlín
This theatre in the Karlín district, near the large Florenc bus station, specialises in American musicals and European operettas.
✉ Křižíkova 10, Praha 8
☎ 24212776
🚇 Florenc

Opera Mozart
Chamber-music concerts, short operas and on Sunday also jazz concerts are performed in this small concert hall.
✉ Novotného lávka 1

Church of St Nicholas
Chamber music concerts are given at the end of the afternoon several times a week in this baroque church in the Lesser Quarter. Mozart's *Requiem* is frequently performed here.
✉ Malostranské náměstí

Laterna Magica
The Czech multimedia shows at the magic lantern – a combination of music, dance, film, theatre, lighting effects and spectacular changes of scenery – captured the world in the 1960s. They are less spectacular these days but still worth a visit.
✉ Národní 4, Praha 1
☎ 249429 🚊 6, 9, 8, 22
🚇 Národní

Národní Divadlo
The neo-Renaissance National Theatre has a mainly Czech programme: operas by Smetana, Dvořák, Janáček, ballet danced to Czech music and Czech theatrical performances.
✉ Národní 2, Praha 1
☎ 24913437
🚊 6, 9, 18, 22
🚇 Národní

Rudolfium
This is the most important concert hall in Prague. It is the home of the world-famous Czech Philharmonic Orchestra and the Prague Radio Symphony Orchestra.
✉ Náměstí Jana Palacha, Praha 1
☎ 24893352
🚇 Staroměstská

Smetanova síň
This concert hall is housed in the Obecní dům and is one of the few art nouveau concert halls in the world. It is the home of the Prague Symphony Orchestra.
✉ Republiky náměstí 5, Praha 1 🚇 Republiky

Státní Opera Praha
Performances in this neo-rococo theatre are exclusively operas by 19th-century foreign composers such as Verdi, Rossini, Puccini, Bizet.
✉ Wilonova 4, Praha 2
☎ 24227693
🚇 Muzeum

Stavovské Divadlo
This is the oldest theatre in Prague where Mozart had the premiere of his opera *Don Giovanni*.

Mozart operas are therefore a fixed part of the programme. Classical and modern plays by Czech and foreign writers are often accompanied by a simultaneous translation into English and/or German.

✉ Ovocny trh, Praha 1

☎ 24215001

🚇 Můstek

Brno
Besední dům

The Community Building is the home of the Brno State Philharmonic Orchestra. The programmes consist mainly of works by Czech composers.

✉ Kamenského náměstí 8

Janáčkovo Divadlo

This theatre, named after Moravia's most important composer, specialises in operas, operettas and ballet.

✉ Sady Osvobození 12

Mahenovo Divadlo

In this beautiful neo-baroque theatre, as well as operettas you can enjoy classic Czech plays.

✉ Divadelní 76

Reduta Divadlo

This is the oldest theatre in Brno and is proud of the fact that Mozart played here in 1767. The programme mainly consists of operettas.

✉ Zelný trh 4

České Budějovice
Dům Kultury & Divadelní sál

Concerts and operettas are performed in the theatre of this modern House of Culture just outside the town.

✉ U tří lvů

Jihočeské Divadlo

The south Bohemian Theatre is mainly the venue for plays but from time to time concerts are held here.

✉ Dr Stejskala 4

Český Krumlov
Městské Divadlo

Classical concerts and Czech plays are performed in this municipal theatre.

✉ Horní 57

Zámecká Divadlo

The splendid rococo theatre on the historic castle square can only be visited when there are performances of concerts or plays. There are musical performances daily during the International Music Festival at the end of July/beginning of August.

✉ ► 16

Zámecká zahrada

During the summer months there are many open-air concerts in the castle's Italian Gardens.

✉ ► 16

Zlín
Dům Umění

This House of Art is the home of the best Czech symphony orchestra, the Bohuslav Martinů Philarmonic Orchestra.

✉ Náměstí T,G, Masaryka 2570

Městské Divadlo

This is the Municipal Theatre specialising in opera and plays. The programme changes each day.

✉ Tomáše Bati 1113

Velké kímo

The 2000-seater Grand Cinema housed in a 1930s building.

Chamber-Music Concerts

Almost every day at the end of the afternoon, usually after 5PM, there is a chamber-music concert somewhere in Prague in a small room in one of the old palaces or in a church. It is a pleasant end to an afternoon that has been developed by the city. The programmes are often advertised in the street and can be obtained from the tourist information office in Old Town Square.

11

Films

The Czech Republic has a rich tradition in the film industry. Many directors, such as Milos Forman and Jiří have created a stir internationally. The film industry has declined since the fall of the Communist regime because it no longer receives state subsidies. But foreign film makers still make use of Czech locations and know-how by filming in Czech studios with Czech personnel. Czech films can be seen in the many cinemas. Special Czech film weeks are held in the huge Velké Kino in Zlín, centre of Czech cartoon films, and in Biograf Kino in Jičín.

Jazz and Pop

Prague

AghaRTA Jazz centrum

A place to listen to Czech and foreign jazz. All music is live. Also houses a jazz shop.

⊠ Krakovská 5, Praha 1
☎ 24212914
🕓 Daily 9PM–2PM
🚇 Muzeum

Klub X

One of the most popular night spots in Prague where you can dance to disco music and also listen to live performers.

⊠ Na Příkopě 15, Praha 1
☎ 24216073
🕓 Mon–Sat 8PM–4AM, Sun 6–12PM
🚇 Můstek

Lucerna Music Bar

A traditional entertainment centre, specialising in Czech pop music, but also includes Beatles and other revivals.

⊠ Vodičkova 36, Praha 1
☎ 24217108
🕓 Daily 7PM–6AM
🚊 3, 9, 14, 24
🚇 Můstek

Reduta Jazz Club

This is certainly the oldest jazz club in Prague. Here Bill Clinton, on an official visit to the Czech republic while US President, played the saxophone in a jam session. The club specialises in Dixieland and swing.

⊠ Národní 20, Praha 1
☎ 24912246
🕓 Daily 9PM
🚊 6, 9, 18, 22
🚇 Národní

Brno

Alterna

A club particularly for students with live jazz concerts every Sunday evening.

⊠ Kounicova 48
🕓 Sun 8PM–1AM

Boby Centrum

A large and very popular disco, a stronghold of pop and rock music, with two bars and a nightclub.

⊠ Sportovní 2
🕓 Fri–Sat 8PM–4AM, Sun 8PM–1AM

Mersey Club

This is a real music pub with noisy live performances by various rock bands and DJs.

⊠ Minská 15
🕓 Daily 4–12PM, Fri–Sat 4PM–2AM

České Budějovice

Kulturní Dům Hroznová

Jazz concerts are held in the summer in this old cultural centre just behind the main square, mainly on Friday and Saturday evenings.

⊠ Hroznová 24

Zlín

Dům Kultury

This House of Culture specialises in folk music and plays, but there are also regular jazz and pop concerts.

⊠ Gahurova 612

Casinos

Prague

Ambassador

This casino forms part of Hotel Ambassador. The usual repertoire is on offer.

⊠ Václavské náměstí 5–7, Praha 1
☎ 24193681
🕓 24hr/day
🚇 Můstek

Brno

Grand Hotel

The smartest hotel in Brno has a casino with all the traditional games.

⊠ Benšova 18
☎ 24280

Activities

Rock Climbing

Děčín

The sandstone rock
formations of the Labské
piscovce on the border with
Germany attract many
climbers at weekends. This
region, also known as 'Little
Switzerland', is however
less spectacular than the
Adršpašsko-Teplicé skály.
The best way to approach
Labské piscovce is from
Děčín (▶ 42).

✉ **Prokopa Holého 8**
☎ **22678**

Trutnov

Climbing steep rocks is a
popular pastime in the
Czech Republic. However,
because Czech mountains
are in the middle range, rock
climbing is less spectacular
than in the Alps.
The rock formations of the
Adršpašsko-Teplicé skály are
the most popular with
climbers. These fantastic
rock formations are the
eastern outliers of the Giant
Mountains (▶ 34). The best
approach to the rock
formations is from the small
town of Trutnov, north of
Hradec Králové (▶ 42).

✉ **Krkonošovo náměstí 72**
☎ **26426**

Jičín

Experienced climbers shrug
their shoulders when the
Česky ráj is mentioned as a
climbing area. They regard
the Bohemian Paradise as
nursery slopes (▶ 40, 114).
However, it is especially
suitable for beginners
led by an old hand. Jičín
is an attractive base
(▶ 40, 96, 104).

✉ **Valdštejnovo náměstí**
☎ **24390**

Cycling

Český Krumlov

The Czech Republic has an
extensive network of cycle
routes. Route maps can be
obtained ffom the Central
Czech Tourist Office (CCC)
and local tourist information
offices.
You will find favourite routes
at the foot of the Šumava
Mountains, along the
Austrian Border and in the
Beskydy district. There is an
attractive cycle route laid out
between Prague and Vienna.
Hiring cycles has not really
taken off, but there is
usually a cycle shop in each
town.
One of the most popular
cycle trips is from Český
Krumlov (▶ 16) to the Lipno
Lake and back. It takes four
to five hours during which
there is quite a climb on the
way out and then a steep
drop to the lake where you
can cool off. The return
journey is nearly all downhill.
You can hire cycles in Česky
Krumlov near Hotel Růže
and also find route maps for
other cycle trips.

✉ **Horní 153**
☎ **711141**

Golf

Prague

Golf has become very
fashionable in the Czech
Republic in recent years and
the number of golf courses
has grown correspondingly.
Whereas in 1990 there were
only two golf courses (in
Prague and Karlovy Vary)
there are now more than 15,
spread throughout the
country. There are, however,
only four international 18-
hole courses, in Karlštejn,

Safety

It is essential to follow the
marked routes if you go
walking in the mountains.
Particularly in the north of
the country, erosion makes
the paths dangerous. If you
stray off the marked path in
areas without tree cover
you can easily trigger stone
or snow avalanches.

Walking/Cycling Routes on the Internet

The website www.kamven.cz/english provides a great deal of useful information for walkers and cyclists, including details of routes, difficulty and equipment required, e.g., mountain bike or touring bike, walking shoes or boots. Most of the basic information has been translated into English. There is also information on local points of interest such as historic sites.

Mariánské Lázně, Olomouc and Ostrava (▶ 43). The Golf Club Prague in Motol has a 9-hole course.

✉ **Na Moráni 4**
☎ **652464**

Tennis

Prague

Tennis is the most popular sport in the Czech Republic after football and ice hockey, as is evident from Czech players' international successes. There are public tennis courts in all towns. The more expensive hotels usually have a court. The largest tennis centre in Prague is on Štvanice Island.

☎ **2324601**
🚊 **3, 8**

Walking

The Czech Republic has about 35,000km of waymarked footpaths. Specialist bookshops and tourist offices sell excellent walking maps.

Český ràj (Bohemian Paradise)

Various footpaths are marked in this area of natural beauty (▶ 40). For a 13km walk take the train from Jičín to Hruba skála, after which follow the yellow route to Trosky Castle and, via the rock mass of Hruboskálské, to the Valdštejn Castle. Return by train to Jičín via Turnov. If you follow the long (32km) red route, you can walk through the Česky Ràj from Jičín to Turnov.

Krkonoše (Giant Mountains)

A very popular route is the Cesta česko–polského

přátelství (Czech–Polish Friendship Path) following the Czech–Polish border. During the Communist regime, Czech and Polish dissidents used the path to meet each other as it runs partly over Polish and partly Czech land. The route begins in the west by the source of the Labe and ends at Horni Malá Úpa. The total length is about 40km but at various points from Harrachov, Špindlerův Mlyn or Pec pod Sněžka you can join the route, with or without taking a cable car or lift. You can stay overnight in a mountain hut (▶ 107).

Šumava

The oldest footpath in the Šumava is Medvědí stezka (the Bear Trail). This is a 14km route that begins in Ovesná, on the south bank of Lake Lipno, and finishes in Černy Kříž (Black Cross) on the edge of the Mrtvy luh (Dead Meadow) nature reserve, an extensive marshy area rich in birds and plants. It is here that the Studená Vltava (Cold Vltava) and the Teplá Vltava join. The trail then continues over the 1,049m-high peak, Pernik.

Water Sports

The many rivers, lakes and reservoirs in the Czech Republic are popular with both locals and tourists for water sports such as sailing, windsurfing, water skiing and canoeing. Boats and canoes can be hired at most water-sports centres.

Český Krumlov

There is a boat-hire firm on the eastern road out of

Horní. From there you can go north on the River Vltava in a canoe or raft to České Budějovce, south to Viššy Brod; both trips are about 35km long. In either direction you will travel through some rapids so it is necessary to wear a helmet. Information can be obtained from the Vltava Travel Agency.

✉ **Kájovska 62**
☎ **711978**
🕐 **Daily 9–5**

Lake Mácha

The 350ha Máchovo jezero, less than 100km north of Prague, is very popular with the city dwellers because of the wide choice of water sports, sandy beaches and forested hills with ruined castles which surround it. It was excavated as a fishpond on the orders of Charles IV about 1360. This Velky Rybník (Great Lake) was named after the most important Czech poet of the 19th-century Romantic Movement, Karel Hynek Mácha (1810–36), who found inspiration for his poetry in the local landscape.

Frýdek Místek

Lake Zermanice, a reservoir, lies about 10km east of the town and is the centre for water sports in the Beskedy region (▶ 12). Equipment is available to hire in Domaslavice (Lake Zermanice) and Staré Hamry (Lake Sace).

Winter Sports

The mountains that enclose the Czech Republic are not the highest in Europe but are suitable for winter sports. Furthermore, there is usually snow for at least three months each winter.

Krkonoše

The Krkonoše are the highest mountains and the busiest winter sports region in the Czech Republic because most pistes descend from here. Špindlerův Mlýn (▶ 19), is the most important centre where the ski area extends between the 715m and 1,310m contours. There are 20 pistes with a total length of 25km, served by 22 ski lifts. There are also various cross-country ski routes marked with a total length of 130km. Pec pod Sněžkou (▶ 19) is the most attractive centre. There are 20 pistes in the area between the 705m and 1,200m contours with a total of 12km and a 22km cross-country ski route. Twenty lifts transport skiers to the upper level.

Šumava

Železná Ruda, on the border with Germany, is the oldest but the best ski area in the South Bohemian Šumava. It is easily reached by train, bus or car and the sports infrastructure is very good. The ski area is at an altitude of 1,000m on the slopes of Špičák Mountain. There is a total of 15km of downhill pistes and a total of 40km of cross-country routes. The winter sports area of Zadov Churáňov lies on the right of the road about halfway between Lenora-Sušice. This area is particularly popular with cross-country skiers and frequently hosts international competitions.

The Czech Republic from the Air

If you want to see the Czech Republic from the air, get in touch with the Aero Club in Jihlava on the motorway between Prague and Brno. In good weather daily flights leave from the airfield for sightseeing trips lasting about an hour.

What's on When

Gold Rush
Once a year the Czech Republic experiences a gold rush. In mid-August people converge on the village of Kestřany, about 8km southwest of the small town of Písek, to pan for gold in the sand of the river Otava. In the past panning for gold was so successful here that the region's fame as a source of gold spread far beyond the national frontiers. Nowadays it is simply a summer outing and many people go to the village to relax and picnic.

19 January
Anniversary of the death of Jan Palach: The suicide in 1969 of the young student who set himself alight in protest at the invasion of Czechoslovakia by the Warsaw Pact countries is commemorated at his memorial in Wenceslas Square.

Mid-February
International Drama Festival in Brno: On about 10 February students from drama and dance schools from central Europe gather in the Moravian Academy of Drama. The festival lasts for a week.

March
International Music Festival: During this month concerts of classical and modern music are performed in venues throughout Prague.

30 April/1 May
Witches' Night: The end of winter is celebrated on the first night of May with a bonfire on Petřin Hill.

May
Theatrale Flora in Olomouc: The most important flower show in the Czech Republic is held during the first week to coincide with the International Festival of Theatre (drama, dance, opera).

May/June
Prague Spring: The great music and dance festival in Prague begins with a procession from Smetana's grave on the Vyšehrad to the concert hall in the Obecni dům that is named after the composer. This is followed by a performance of his best-known work, *Má Vlast* (*My Homeland*).

End of June
Strážnice Festival: One of the greatest festivals of folk culture in Europe. People flock to the village over the three days of the festival.

June/July
Smetana Festival in Litomysl: For two weeks Smetana's operas are performed in his birthplace. The performances take place in the concert hall of the castle opposite the museum/birthplace of the composer.

Beginning of July
Film Festival at Karlovy Vary: Together with Cannes, Berlin and Venice this is one of the biggest film festivals in Europe. Over ten days about 200 feature films and documentaries are shown. The atmosphere is much more informal than at the other festivals – cheaper and accessible to the general public.

End of September
Spectaculo interesse in Ostrava: This week-long international puppet festival is held in the Divadlo loutek.

October
Mozart in Prague: Mozart is commemorated over the whole month with many concerts and opera performances.

December
Christmas Markets: Markets are held around Christmas time in many Czech towns. The biggest is on Wenceslas Square in Prague.

Practical Matters

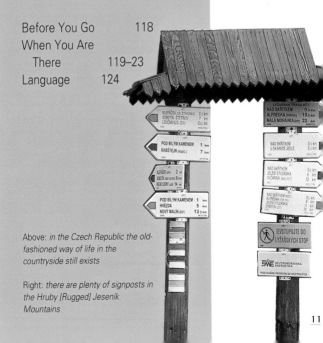

Above: *in the Czech Republic the old-fashioned way of life in the countryside still exists*

Right: *there are plenty of signposts in the Hruby [Rugged] Jeseník Mountains*

11

TIME DIFFERENCES

GMT	Czech Rep.	Germany	USA (NY)	Netherlands	Spain
12 noon	1PM	1PM	7AM	1PM	1PM

BEFORE YOU GO

WHAT YOU NEED

		UK	Germany	USA	Netherlands	Spain
● Required ○ Suggested ▲ Not required	Some countries require a passport to remain valid for a minimum period (usually at least six months) beyond the date of entry – contact their consulate or embassy or your travel agent for details.					
Passport/National Identity Card		●	●	●	●	●
Visa		▲	▲	▲	▲	▲
Onward or Return Ticket		▲	▲	▲	▲	▲
Health Inoculations		▲	▲	▲	▲	▲
Health Documentation (➤ 123, Health)		●	●	●	●	●
Travel Insurance		○	○	○	○	○
Driving Licence (national)		●	●	●	●	●
Car Insurance Certificate		●	●	●	●	●
Car Registration Document		●	●	●	●	●

WHEN TO GO

Prague

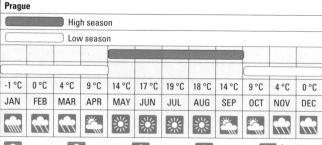

High season

Low season

-1 °C	0 °C	4 °C	9 °C	14 °C	17 °C	19 °C	18 °C	14 °C	9 °C	4 °C	0 °C
JAN	FEB	MAR	APR	MAY	JUN	JUL	AUG	SEP	OCT	NOV	DEC

 Very wet   Wet   Cloud   Sun   Sunshine & showers

TOURIST OFFICES

In the UK
Czech Tourist Authority,
The Czech Centre,
95 Great Portland Street,
London W1N 5RA
☎ 020 7291 9920
Fax: 020 7436 8300

In the USA
Czech Tourist Authority,
1109–1111 Madison Avenue,
New York
NY 10028
☎ 212/288 0830
Fax: 212/288 0971

POLICE 158

FIRE 150

AMBULANCE 155

WHEN YOU ARE THERE

ARRIVING

Czechoslovak Airlines – ČSA (☎ 24104111) operates direct scheduled flights to Prague from Britain, mainland Europe and North America. Flight time from London is two hours. Prague is connected by rail to all main European capitals (► 121, Public Transport).

Praha Ruzyně Airport Kilometres to city centre	**Journey times**
● ━━━ **20 km** ━━━ ▶	🚌 40 minutes
	🚍 35 minutes
	🚕 20–25 minutes

Praha Hlavní Station In city centre	**Journey times**
● ━━━ ▶	🚌 on metro line C
	🚍 available
	🚕 available

MONEY

The monetary unit of the Czech Republic is the Koruna česká (Kč) – or Czech crown – which is divided into 100 haléř (h) – or heller – though you will not find many of the latter. There are coins of 10, 20 and 50 hellers and 1, 2, 5, 10, 20 and 50 crowns. Banknotes come in 20, 50, 100, 200, 500, 1,000 and 5,000 crowns. Money may be changed at the airport, in banks (► 120, Opening Hours), major hotels, Čedok offices, and in the centre of Prague at exchange offices. It is an offence to change money through street black-market money dealers; in any case, they rarely offer an attractive rate.

TIME

The Czech Republic is on Central European Time (GMT+1), but from late March, when clocks are put forward one hour, until late October, Czech Summer Time (GMT+2) operates.

CUSTOMS

YES

Duty Free Limits:
Alcohol – spirits: 1L *and* wine: 2L
Cigarettes: 200 *or*
Cigarillos: 100 *or*
Cigars: 50 *or*
Tobacco: 250gms *or*
a proportionate combination of the above tobacco products.
You must be 18 and over to benefit from the alcohol and tobacco allowance.
Perfume: 50ml *or*
Toilet water: 250ml
Gifts: not in excess of 3,000Kč per person.
Fuel: 10L in a spare can (for personal use).

NO

Drugs, firearms, ammunition, offensive weapons, obscene material, unlicensed animals.

CONSULATES

UK
☎ 24510439

Germany
☎ 24510323

USA
☎ 24510847

Netherlands
☎ 24510189

Spain
☎ 24311441

WHEN YOU ARE THERE

TOURIST OFFICES

**Czech Tourist Authority
(Česká centrálna cestovního)**
● Náradní třída 37
   11001 Praha 1
   ☎/Fax: 24211458

Prague
● Prague Information Service
   (Pražská informační služba
   PIS)
   Na příkopě 20
   Nové Město, Praha 1
   ☎ 264022 or 544444
   🅜 Můstek or Republiky

Brno
● Kulturní a informační
   centrum
   Radnická 8
   ☎ 42211090

Český Krumlov
● Infocentrum
   Náměstí Svornosti 1
   ☎ 711183

Karlovy Vary
● Kur-info
   Vřídelní Colonnade
   ☎ 3224097

Olomouc
● Olomoucká informační
   služba OIS
   Horní náměstí 1
   ☎ 5513385

Plzeň
● Town Information Service
   (Městské informační
   středisko)
   Náměstí Republiky 41
   ☎ 7236535

NATIONAL HOLIDAYS

J	F	M	A	M	J	J	A	S	O	N	D
1		(1)	(1)	2		2				1	3

1 Jan	New Year's Day
Mar/Apr	Easter Monday
1 May	May Day
8 May	Liberation Day
5 Jul	St Cyril and St Methodius Day
6 Jul	Jan Hus Day
28 Oct	Independence Day
24 Dec	Christmas Eve
25 Dec	Christmas Day
26 Dec	St Stephen's Day

On these days banks, offices, department stores and
some shops close. However, restaurants, museums
and other tourist attractions tend to stay open.

OPENING HOURS

○ Shops   ● Churches
● Offices   ● Museums
● Banks   ● Pharmacies

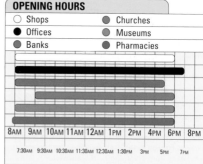

8AM	9AM	10AM	11AM	12AM	1PM	2PM	4PM	6PM	8PM

7:30AM   9:30AM   10:30AM   11:30AM   12:30AM   1:30PM   3PM   5PM   7PM

Large department stores, supermarkets and shops in
tourist centres often have longer opening hours,
particularly in the summer. Pharmacies, banks and
shops are generally closed on Saturday afternoon.
From October to May banks are open until 4.30PM,
but from June to September are closed on Saturday.
The opening times for museums given here are
merely an indication; some museums are open
longer hours in summer than in winter. Some
museums are closed for a day at the weekend
or during the week, usually on Monday.

**DRIVE ON THE
RIGHT**

**TOILETS
CHARGE**

PUBLIC TRANSPORT

Internal Flights Czechoslovak Airlines (ČSA), Revoluční 1, Praha 1 (☎ 2317395), and a variety of other carriers link Prague with Brno and Ostrava. Though not cheap, especially when compared with the train or bus, they are useful when you want to get somewhere quickly.

Trains Czech Railways (Československé Staní Dráhy ČSD) run *rychlík* which stop only at major towns, and *osobní* calling at every station. Services to North and East Bohemia and North Moravia depart from Masary Station (Masarykovo nádraží), to South Bohemia and South Moravia from Smíchovské nádraží, to North and West Bohemia from Nádraží Holešovice.

Buses The quickest way to travel through the Czech Republic on public transport is to use the buses run by the Czech Bus Company (Česká automobilová doprava, ČSAD). Buses generally run more frequently than trains, serve more places – even remote ones – and are scarcely more expensive. In Prague buses leave from the bus stations Florenc, Anděl, Palmovka or Holešovice to all destinations.

Metro The metro is the fastest and most comfortable means of public transport in Prague. It is possible to reach all the suburbs of Prague via one of the three lines A (green), B (yellow) and C (red) that cross at one point in the centre so that changing is simple. They run from 5AM to midnight, every 2 minutes at peak times, otherwise every 5 to 10 minutes. Tickets are inexpensive and single/multi-day tickets are also available. The letter 'M' with a downward arrow marks a station entrance. A disadvantage is that you do not see the city.

CAR RENTAL

The big international firms have offices at Prague airport where you can book a car directly or through your travel agent (necessary in high season). The biggest Czech firm is Czechocar, with offices in all the larger towns.

TAXIS

There are taxis in most Czech towns and cities. You can find them in taxi ranks, hail them in the street or call them by telephone. Privatisation has led to stiff competition. Agree a price and make sure the meter is connected. Registered taxis should have a meter clearly displayed.

DRIVING

Speed limit on motorways (annual toll payable): **110kph.** Minimum limit: **50kph**

Speed limit on country roads: **90kph**

Speed limit on urban roads: **60kph**

Must be worn in front seats – and rear seats where fitted. Under 12s may not travel in the front seat.

Don't drink *any* alcohol if driving. The allowed blood/alcohol level is zero and penalties are severe.

Petrol (*benzín*) is sold in leaded form as *special* (91 octane) and super (96 octane). Unleaded petrol comes as *natural* (95 octane) and *super plus* (98 octane); the latter is available only at larger petrol stations. Diesel (*nafta*) is also available. In Prague, filling stations are few and far between, but some open 24 hours.

ÚAMK, the Czech automobile club, operates a 24-hour nationwide breakdown service on the same terms as your own motoring club (non-members pay in full), ☎ 0123 (123 in Prague) or 154 from mobile phones. On motorways use emergency phones (every 2km) to summon help.

Scale ruler markings:

CENTIMETRES
0 1 2 3 4 5 6 7 8

INCHES
0 1 2 3

PERSONAL SAFETY

The Czech Republic is a relatively safe country, although with the rapid increase in tourism petty crime has risen especially in Prague. Take particular care in places popular with tourists. Report any loss or theft to the police.

- Watch your bag in tourist areas.
- Never leave anything of value visible in your car.
- Leave passports and valuables in the hotel safe.
- Avoid walking alone in dark alleys at night.

Police assistance:
☎ **158**
from any call box

TELEPHONE

There are public telephones on the street and near metro stations in Prague. Older orange phones, accepting only 1Kč coins, are solely for local calls.

Grey phones take 1, 2, 5 and 10Kč coins. In the bigger cities there are an increasing number of phonecard (*Telefonní karta*) booths. Buy cards for 100, 190 and 280Kč from post offices, tobacconists and newsagents. The code for Prague is 02.

International Dialling Codes	
From Czech Republic to:	
UK:	00 44
USA:	00 1
Germany:	00 49
Netherlands:	00 31
Spain:	00 34

POST

Post Offices have distinctive *Pošta* signs outside. They are generally open from 8AM to 7PM (Saturday to 12 noon, closed on Sunday). The main post office in Prague at Jindřišská 14, Nové Město is open 24 hours.

ELECTRICITY

The power supply in the Czech Republic is 220 volts.

Plugs are of the two-round-pin variety, so an adaptor is needed for most non-Continental European appliances and a voltage transformer for appliances operating on 100–120 volts.

TIPS/GRATUITIES

Yes ✓ No ✗		
Hotels	✗	
Restaurants	✓	10%
Cafés	✓	10%
Taxis	✓	10%
Tour guides	✓	(20Kč)
Porters	✓	(40Kč)
Usherettes	✗	
Hairdressers	✓	10%
Cloakroom attendants	✓	(2Kč)
Toilets	✓	(2Kč)

HEALTH

Insurance
Emergency medical treatment is free to foreign visitors to the Czech Republic. Nationals of EU countries are entitled to additional medical care (show passport). Private medical insurance is advised (essential for all other visitors).

Dental Services
Dental treatment must be paid for. Ask for a receipt as proof of payment when you return home. If you require urgent treatment in Prague there is an Emergency Dental Crisis Helpline (☎ 1097).

Sun Advice
The sunniest and warmest period is between June and August. The temperature can then climb to about 30°C, especially in south Moravia. There are often frequent thunderstorms that cool the atmosphere. If the sun is fierce apply a sunscreen and wear a hat, or go to a museum.

Drugs
Pharmacies (*lékárnat* or *apothéka*) are the only places to sell over-the-counter medicines. They also dispense many drugs (*leky*) normally available only on prescription in other Western countries.

Safe Water
It is not advisable to drink tap water as it is loaded with toxins and heavily chlorinated. Still bottled table water (*Stolní pitní voda*) is the most common.

CONCESSIONS

Students/Young people Holders of an International Student Identity Card (ISIC) are entitled to a 50 per cent reduction at museums and galleries in some big cities, including Prague.

Student cards also offer reductions on international trains, though not on domestic public transport. The ČKM (Czech Youth Travel Agency), Žitna 12, Praha 2 (☎ 299454), specialises in cheap travel for young people and students in and outside the Czech Republic. It also issues ISICs.

Senior Citizens There are no special concessions for senior citizens.

CLOTHING SIZES

UK	USA	Czech Republic		
36	36	46		
38	38	48		
40	40	50		Suits
42	42	52		
44	44	54		
46	46	56		
8	7	41		
8.5	7.5	42		
9.5	8.5	43		Shoes
10.5	9.5	44		
11.5	10.5	45		
12	11	46		
14.5	14.5	37		
15	15	38		
15.5	15.5	39/40		Shirts
16	16	41		
16.5	16.5	42		
17	17	43		
6	8	34		
8	10	36		
10	12	38		Dresses
12	14	40		
14	16	42		
16	18	44		
6	4.5	38		
6.5	5	38		
7	5.5	39		Shoes
7.5	6	39		
8	6.5	40		
8.5	7	41		

- Contact the airline at least 72 hours before departure to reconfirm your booking to prevent being 'bumped' from that plane because of over-allocation.
- There is an airport departure tax which is normally included in the cost of the ticket.
- Antiques can only be exported with a certificate, issued by the National Museum or National Gallery, indicating the object is not of Czech national heritage.

LANGUAGE

The official language of the Czech Republic is Czech (Český) – a highly complex western Slav tongue. Czech sounds and looks daunting, but apart from a few special letters, each letter and syllable is pronounced as it is written – the key is always to stress the first syllable of a word.

Any attempt to speak Czech will be heartily appreciated although English is spoken by many involved in the tourist trade. Below are a few Czech words that may be helpful.

hotel	*hotel*	toilet	*záchod/WC*
room	*pokoj*	bath	*koupelnoou*
I would like a room	*potřebuji pokoje*	shower	*sprcha*
... single/double	*... jednolůžový/ dvoulůžkový*	cold/hot water	*studená/teplá voda*
... for one night	*... na jednu noc*	towel	*ručník*
how much per night?	*kolik stojí jedna noc?*	soap	*mýdlo*
		room number	*císlo pokoje*
reservation	*reservaci*	key	*klíč*
breakfast	*snídaně*		

bank	*banku*	cheap	*levný*
post office	*pošta*	expensive	*drahý*
foreign exchange	*směnárna*	free (no charge)	*zdarma*
Czech crown	*koruna česká (kč)*	more	*více*
heller	*haléř*	less	*méně*
credit card	*credit card*	the bill	*účet*
how much?	*kolik?*	it's a rip off!	*to je zlodějina!*

restaurant	*restaurace*	lunch	*oběd*
coffee house	*kavárna*	dinner	*večeře*
pub	*hospoda*	starter	*předkrm*
wine bar	*vinárna*	main course	*hlavní jídlo*
table	*stůl*	dish of the day	*nabídka dne*
menu	*jídelní lístek*	dessert	*moučnik*
fixed-price menu	*standardní menu*	waiter	*čišník*
wine list	*nápojový lístek*	waitress	*servírka*

aeroplane	*letadlo*	pleasure steamer	*parník*
airport	*letiště*	small boat	*lodička*
train	*vlak*	ticket	*lístek*
train station	*nádraží*	... single/return	*jednosměrnou/ zpáteční*
metro station	*stanice*		
bus	*autobus*	... first/second class	*první/druhou třídu*
bus station	*autobusové nádraží*	ticket office	*pokladna*
tram	*tramvaj*	seat reservation	*místenka*
bus/tram stop	*zastávka*		

yes	*ano*	excuse me	*promiňte*
no	*ne*	sorry	*pardon*
please	*prosím*	help!	*pomoc!*
thank you	*děkuji*	today	*dnes*
hello	*ahoj*	yesterday	*včera*
goodbye	*na shledanou*	tomorrow	*zítra*
good morning	*dobré ráno*	open	*otevřeno*
goodnight	*dobrou noc*	closed	*zavřeno*

Acknowledgements
Kosmos-Z&K and the Automobile Association wishes to thank the following photographers, libraries, associations and museums for their assistance in the preparation of this book:
CZECH TOURIST AUTHORITY 6a, 7a, 18, 19, 21, 23, 24, 27b, 43, 44, 47a, 50a, 52, 54, 55, 58, 67, 76, 77, 90; **DAVID LINDSAY** 6b, 34, 35, 91a; **GERARD OP HET VELD** 5a, 9b, 15b, 17, 20, 22a, 37, 40, 42, 46, 47b, 50b, 51, 53a, 63, 64, 68, 69, 72, 73, 75, 78, 79, 80, 81, 82, 83, 84, 85, 86, 87, 88, 89, 117b, 122; **HENJA SCHNEIDER** 22b, 26, 41, 56; **JAN BURGAU (courtesy Uitgeverij Bert Bakker)** 14; **KEES-WILLEM KARSSEN** 5b; **MARCEL QUARTEL** 2, 25a, 27a, 45, 60, 66, 70, 71, 91b, 117a; **PAUL SMIT** 1, 15a, 28, 29, 32, 33, 36, 38, 48, 53b; **PAUL VAN GALEN** 8, 9a, 12, 13a, 16, 49, 57, 61, 62, 65.

The remaining photographs are from the Association's own library (AA PHOTO LIBRARY) with contributions from:
S MCBRIDE b/c; **C SAWYER** f/c (top c, f, g, bottom); **J WYAND** f/c (top a, b, d, e); 7b, 39, 65, 74.

Dear Essential Traveller

**Your comments, opinions and recommendations are very
important to us. So please help us to improve our travel
guides by taking a few minutes to complete this simple
questionnaire.**

*You do not need a stamp (unless posted outside the UK). If you do not want to cut this page
from your guide, then photocopy it or write your answers on a plain sheet of paper.*

Send to: **The Editor, AA World Travel Guides,
FREEPOST SCE 4598, Basingstoke RG21 4GY.**

Your recommendations…

We always encourage readers' recommendations for restaurants, nightlife
or shopping – if your recommendation is used in the next edition of the
guide, we will send you a *FREE* **AA** *Essential* **Guide** of your choice.
Please state below the establishment name, location and your reasons
for recommending it.

_____
_____
_____
_____

Please send me **AA** *Essential* _____
(*see list of titles inside the front cover*)

About this guide…

Which title did you buy?
    AA *Essential* _____
Where did you buy it?_____
When? m m / y y

Why did you choose an AA *Essential* Guide? _____
_____
_____
_____
_____

Did this guide meet your expectations?
    Exceeded ☐ Met all ☐ Met most ☐ Fell below ☐
    Please give your reasons_____
_____
_____
_____

continued on next page…
continued on next page…

Were there any aspects of this guide that you particularly liked? _____

_____

_____

_____

Is there anything we could have done better? _____

_____

_____

_____

_____

About you…

Name (*Mr/Mrs/Ms*) _____

Address _____

_____

_____ Postcode _____

Daytime tel nos _____

Which age group are you in?

Under 25 ☐   25–34 ☐   35–44 ☐   45–54 ☐   55–64 ☐   65+ ☐

How many trips do you make a year?

Less than one ☐   One ☐   Two ☐   Three or more ☐

Are you an AA member? Yes ☐   No ☐

About your trip…

When did you book? m m / y y   When did you travel? m m / y y

How long did you stay? _____

Was it for business or leisure? _____

Did you buy any other travel guides for your trip?

If yes, which ones? _____

_____

Thank you for taking the time to complete this questionnaire. Please send
it to us as soon as possible, and remember, you do not need a stamp
(*unless posted outside the UK*).

Happy Holidays!